The Philosophy
of the Social
Sciences

For Robin and Mus

Vernon Pratt

The Philosophy
of the Social
Sciences

ROUTLEDGE
London and New York

First published in 1978
by Methuen & Co Ltd

Reprinted in 1989 and 1991
by Routledge
11 New Fetter Lane, London EC4P 4EE

Simultaneously published in the USA and Canada
by Routledge
a division of Routledge, Chapman and Hall, Inc.
29 West 35th Street, New York, NY 10001

© 1978 Vernon Pratt

Typeset by Red Lion Setters, London
and printed in Great Britain at the
University Printing House, Cambridge

ISBN 0-415-04288-7

Contents

Preface

I have written this book very deliberately for people to whom philosophy as an academic subject is unfamiliar, in the belief that they are missing something important. The person I have had in mind is the student of social 'science', not ill disposed towards philosophy as broadly conceived, but often developing an entrenched hostility when detail and manner of argument, no matter how misleadingly, create a sense of irritating and burdensome irrelevance. What I should like to have done is to have combined simplicity and a stress on the big issues behind the detailed argumentation with the rigour and precision that are the major strengths of recent Anglo-Saxon philosophy. But with writers of modest powers such as my own these objectives *compete* for attention, and I am more than conscious of the likelihood of having paid for intelligibility (though never intentionally, I may say) with vagueness and oversimplification. I have taken two steps to ameliorate the situation: first, by leaving issues open, I have tried to make the point that a great deal of detailed argumentation must intervene between a reading of my introduction of an issue and arriving at a properly defensible conclusion upon it; and, second, I have tried to point at every stage to other reading which would take the argument further.

Choosing the words that follow, and deciding on their best order, has taken a ridiculously long time, and consequently has involved the indulgence and relied on the help of a disproportionate number of people. As the book finally goes to press I find my memory unequal to the task of reliably identifying those — mostly students —

who through their kindness and encouragement must bear responsibility for its existence and therefore, since I have done my best, for its shortcomings. But my reminiscing does throw up upon the screen of consciousness the figures of two former colleagues, Barry Wilkins and Andrew Belsey — amiable, helpful and encouraging critics both; and two set in authority, Lyn Evans and Tom McPherson, to whom I am grateful for kindly and unstinting support. I have also to thank Gillian Roberts and Christine Pearcy for their generous help in preparing the manuscript, and Panda and Tom Pratt, who have struggled, though not always successfully, to keep this book in its place.

Acknowledgements

The author and publishers would like to thank the following for permission to reproduce the illustrations which appear in this book: the New York Public Library (Print Collection) for the Albrecht Dürer engraving of a rhinoceros (1515), Emil Schulthess for his photograph of the African rhinoceros, and E. H. Gombrich for his arrangement of the rhinoceros illustrations; Hodder and Stoughton Educational for Plate IX of *Applications of Nuclear Physics* (1964); and *University of California Publications in Psychology* for E. C. Tolman and C. H. Honzik's apparatus to test for the learning by insight in the rat (1930).

1 Introduction

The way we study people will reflect what we take them to be; so that at the outset of social study we have to make up our minds on the question we should really like to hold over until the end: what is the nature of the human being, and what sort of a thing is the society to which the individual belongs? Is the human being essentially a rather complicated machine, as some have suggested? If so, we surely have to try to understand how it works in the same way that we try to understand the workings of a computer or a chemical factory. Or does the fact that we are *conscious*, and perhaps that we exercise *free will* and recognize a realm of *values*, render the mechanical approach entirely misleading?

Alternatively, it may be that social study should proceed on the basis that the human being is really just an *animal*, and should requisition the methods that have demonstrated their appropriateness in the case of sticklebacks and geese. Or, thinking perhaps of the fact that the naked ape is not too embarrassed to *talk* in an apparently uniquely sophisticated way, we may be tempted by the view that people are neither machines merely, nor animals, but of their own kind — creatures apart; and that to understand them we cannot simply transfer the concepts and methodology that may be useful for other purposes.

A similar range of possibilities presents itself when we begin to think of studying the groups that people make up. Is a society something over and above the individuals it comprises? Are we to think of it as like a building, or as like a machine, or as like a living organism? Or is it nothing other than a loose association of individuals?

Questions such as these, about the fundamental character of human beings and human groups, have to be confronted in any reflective study of human life — and at the outset. They cannot, unfortunately, be settled by any simple appeal to accumulated evidence; for they represent rival approaches to social study, and one cannot conduct inquiries in an attempt to discover the approach that is most appropriate without, in fact, *adopting* some such approach and thus to some extent prejudicing any conclusion.

If I say now that it is this situation that provides part of the occasion for the present book, I must immediately repudiate the suggestion that the best approach to the study of man is properly to be discovered by philosophical thought. I would simply say that the issue of the nature of the human being and the human group has philosophical dimensions. Factual evidence is of essential importance — but so is the interpretation of it. And in that difficult but inescapable task one's thinking will benefit from being clear and profound as well as informed.

Adopting an orientation does not, however, settle *every* philosophical issue that arises in connection with social study. There still arise, for example, different conceptions of how theories can be obtained from facts, different views, indeed, as to whether there *are* such things as facts. It is difficult to say what makes these topics, and the others that appear in my list of contents, peculiarly 'philosophical', and hence to justify their appearance within the covers of one book. What unites them perhaps is their peculiar difficulty, the fact that, though they inevitably arise in any reflective study of people and society, there seems no obvious, straightforward way of working towards their solution. But they are also, I believe, *important*; for even the more abstract problems I attempt to raise (and this is why I have chosen to raise them) have implications for the conduct of social study, and therefore for its findings, and thus for the action, individual and collective, it will seem rational to engage in.

2 Man as a machine

1 *Introduction*

Stand man up against most artificial machines and he will be seen to be a creature of very impressive powers. He can read and write as well as speak and understand; he can calculate, remember, selectively forget; he can imagine, ponder, solve highly difficult theoretical and practical problems; he can write and respond to poetry, create and enjoy music; and so on.

Paradoxically, however, one of the most spectacular recent manifestations of his intelligence has been the design and construction of *machines* which are beginning to rival him in even some of his more sophisticated abilities. Of course it's early days yet; but already the early detractors of these extraordinarily impressive devices have been forced to think again. 'It used to be possible', Donald Michie reminds us, 'to sweep the social challenge of computers under the carpet with the dismissive phrase "high speed morons".' But he goes on: 'Today, however, computers play draughts at a good club standard, solve difficult problems in logic, compose dull but passable music, out-perform librarians in the relevant retrieval of certain classes of document, translate Russian into useful dog-English, and perform many other exacting tasks of a non-numerical nature.'

These developments, so some say, make it increasingly difficult to deny the mechanical conception of man. He may be very much more complex in his organization than even our most advanced artificial devices, it is granted, but it begins to be undeniable that the human being is simply a robot, the body, controlled by a computer, the brain.

We begin by considering this mechanical conception of man because there are at present very influential approaches to the study of human beings which *apparently*, at any rate, assume its validity: behaviourism is perhaps the most striking example.

2   *Cartesian mechanism*

Although, as I have suggested, it is easy to see recent developments in cybernetics, and in computer technology in particular, as establishing the case for 'mechanical' man, the idea itself is almost as old as the hills. Cybernetics has certainly given it a new impetus, but it is an idea that goes in a sense right back to Democritus and Epicurus in ancient Greece.

One of the most interesting and important ancestors of today's mechanists, however, was the French thinker René Descartes. Descartes's mechanism was restricted to animals, and the sense in which he regarded them as machines seems relatively straightforward. For him, to say something was a machine was to say it was an unconscious robot; and his claim was simply that this was what animals *were*: unconscious robots, whose internal mechanism was based on the principles of the pump and the lever and the cog-wheel which man was learning at that time to exploit so effectively in artificial engines.

The reason why Descartes restricted his thesis to animals is obvious if we bear in mind the fact that he laid great stress in his general philosophy on man's *consciousness*. The fact that a man *thought*, was *conscious* of himself doing things, was *aware* of his own existence — this he took to be the one great certainty upon which the entire edifice of knowledge would have to be built. Clearly, then, if for Descartes 'being a machine' meant being an unconscious robot, he could not call *man* a machine. For that would be to claim that man was an unconscious robot, and in a sense the most basic fact about man, thought Descartes, was that he was *conscious*. So his thesis had to be that, if animals were machines, men were different.

A central problem in trying to understand the *modern* claim that man is a machine now stands out clearly. For surely the mechanist today does not wish to deny that man is conscious; yet he *does* want to claim that man is a 'machine'. We must conclude that he cannot be using the word in Descartes's sense. And from that conclusion the difficult question arises: in what sense, then, *is* he using it? What is the sense of 'machine' when it is claimed in the contemporary context that 'man is a machine'?

3 *Determinism*

We are helped towards an answer by those who denounce the doctrine — as some with great passion do — as a piece of mischief. To think of man as a machine, they say, is to degrade him, to treat him as much less important, much less significant, much less valuable than in fact he is. Objectors such as these find the meaning of the doctrine clear enough to take unambiguous exception to it. How then are they understanding it? There are in fact a number of different kinds of objectors; but to begin with I wish to point to just two.

3.1 *A religious objection.* First, let us consider the viewpoint of the orthodox Christian, and just one of the several objections that might be raised from there.

It might be said that the whole of Christian theology hangs on the proposition that man is capable of responding to the love of God. Man was created, it is said, as a free, independent being, and by his own choice fell into evil ways — evil ways from which the love of God, expressed in the life and death of Jesus Christ, can rescue him. Again, though, the rescue is dependent on man's free, responsible and independent response: he must himself grasp the rope that is thrown to him or he is lost. And if you ask a Christian (of this mainstream belief) why it was necessary for God to endow his creatures with free will in the first place, the answer will be that the 'love' of a zombie is of no value to God: He had no use for the obedience of one who *could not but* obey Him.

Now it seems that when the religious person hears us say that man is a machine, he takes us to be denying that man is 'free' in the sense indicated. A machine, he assumes, is by its very nature incapable of freely willed responses. It *reacts* to changes in its surroundings, certainly, but *choice* or *decision* cannot enter in. It reacts in a completely determined way, according to the rigid laws of physical nature. Think of a car engine — a straightforward example of an artificial device. The engine certainly reacts to pressure on its accelerator; but there's no question of its *deciding* to rev up, or of its *choosing* just how much to do so. Other things being equal, it revs up to exactly the same level every time the accelerator is depressed by a given amount. And the level is determined simply by the mechanical properties of the system.

We are invited to contrast this *mechanical* behaviour with what we know of men's behaviour. What a man does, it is claimed, is not determined by the physical environment in which he finds himself at any particular time. He may find himself in the same physical environment on two successive days, for instance, and yet behave differently on each occasion. The first time he chooses to do one thing, the second time he chooses to do another.

Thus, because it depends on the freedom of choice indicated here, mainstream Christian theology is attacked by mechanism; and that is the first source of objection to it.

3.2 *An ethical objection.*   The second, based on ethical considerations, is not much different. Again it is assumed that to regard a man as a machine is to regard him as a robot, lacking the ability to make freely willed decisions or to determine his own actions by conscious rational choice. But where the theologian protested that a being of this kind could not make a religious response to God, the present objector's worry is that this kind of robot-being could not behave *ethically*. Ethical concepts would simply not apply to him.

The point here is that ethical concepts are held to carry with them the implication of choice or free decision on the part of the agent in question. We cannot, for example, be *blamed* for something we could not avoid doing. We can only have *duties* or *obligations* to do things that lie within our power. We cannot *praise* someone for doing something which he could not help doing.

You have only to think of the situations with which a court of law is sometimes presented to realize the force of this point. A defendant will often call a psychiatrist to speak on his behalf; and what the psychiatrist argues is that the defendant's action was partly or wholly beyond his (the latter's) control. Unless he was somehow to blame for exposing himself to the original infection, no one would dream of holding a flu victim responsible for his own rise in temperature. The psychiatrist argues that the particular crime in question is like the rise in temperature — the product of a particular condition, the symptom, or consequence, of a disease, and therefore beyond the agent's control.

Our point is simply that *if* the psychiatrist makes out his case, convincing us that the accused in real terms had no control over what happened, we regard him as exempt from responsibility. He could not have helped what happened, and therefore he cannot be blamed for it.

What the doctrine that man is a machine does, so it is argued, is to look on *all* human behaviour as beyond our control in the same way. If man is a machine then we have the same control over our actions as the flu victim has over his temperature — that is to say, we have *no* control. We can be held responsible for nothing, blamed for nothing, praised for nothing. It is senseless to tell anyone what he *ought* to do, since he can in no way deviate from the rails of physical necessity. He can have no duties, since he has not the liberty either to obey or disobey. In a word, it does not make sense to apply ethical concepts to machines; and the objection concludes by appealing to the unacceptability of ceasing to apply them to man.

3.3 *Freedom.* The idea that both religious and ethical objections ascribe to mechanism seems to be that man is, if not an *unconscious* robot, a *robot* none the less: made up ultimately of physical parts (the neutrons, protons, electrons and other 'elementary particles' studied by physics) whose law-governed interaction determines the behaviour of the system as a whole. On this conception, what a man does must be considered to be determined not by his own free will but by a causal sequence that stretches indefinitely back into the past.

For example, in my naïvety I may think that whether I go to Cardiff this weekend is still unsettled. Tomorrow, I think to myself, I shall decide, but so far I've not quite made up my mind. The mechanist, on the present conception, is accused of implying that to think in this way is to be deluded. To hold that man is a machine is to hold that his behaviour is determined by causal interactions of his physical parts, and this implies that whether I go to Cardiff or not is *already* settled, *already* determined: it was already settled days, weeks, years ago — in fact it was already settled no matter how far back you go into the past.

Many people have, of course, maintained that this conception of a 'machine' held true at least for inanimate physical systems. A crystal, a cloud or a mountain, being composed of elementary physical parts interacting causally according to fixed principles, were thought of as behaving in a way that was precisely determined by the properties of the particles, their arrangement in space, and the forces exerted by other particles upon them. To those who thought further that absolutely *everything* in the universe was made up in this way of small particles, the argument went further: *everything* that happened was precisely determined beforehand.

A striking implication of this view is that, since what is to happen in the future is settled already, it should be possible in principle to predict it. We should have to know about the way the world is at present, and we should have to know the laws by which things changed. But knowing these two things should enable us, if the view is right, to predict the way the world will be tomorrow, or next year. We should be able to say perfectly precisely what will happen. The megalomania of the idea, as one might almost call it, comes across well in a passage by the nineteenth-century mathematician, Pierre Laplace:

> An intelligence knowing all the forces acting in nature at a given instant, as well as the momentary positions of all things in the universe, would be able to comprehend in one single formula the motions of the largest bodies as well as of the lightest atoms in the world, provided that its intellect were sufficiently powerful to subject all data to analysis: to it nothing would be uncertain, the future as well as the past would be present to its eyes.

4 *Indeterminism*

We have to note, however, though it makes thinking about the topic much more difficult, that the theory of the physical world which underlies this manifesto has passed away — dying when classical physics yielded to quantum theory and withdrew to the periphery of approximation. Instead of the Laplacean notion of a universe whose state was precisely determined by, and calculable from a precise knowledge of, the state that preceded it, we now have a new set of notions with which in many ways we have yet to come to terms.

The tenet that is of most concern in the present context is that at the level of 'elementary particles' some events are conceived of (by orthodox physicists) as happening *without a cause*: they happen, but their occurrence cannot be related causally to any other occurrence.

This implies that at its most basic level reality behaves in a way that displays an element of randomness; with the result that not even the simplest physical systems are subject to precise predictions. We are always, in the nature of things, to some extent uncertain as to what a thing will do next.

So long as one is dealing with relatively large-scale objects, however, statistics usually come to the rescue. For the *aggregate* behaviour of numbers of *individually* random events *can* be predicted, and the greater the numbers, the more reliable the prediction. The fact that everyday objects are made up of such very enormous numbers of elementary particles is therefore responsible for their relatively staid ways.

It has been argued, however, that some ways of organizing the basic building blocks of which complex things are made could result in the randomness of the micro-level being *amplified* (instead of nullified) at the macro-level; and that this is indeed what happens in the case of those physical systems we call *organisms*. Predictability would then *decrease*, with increasing complexity of this special kind of organization, with the result that the behaviour of an extremely sophisticated organism like the human being could be predicted in only the sketchiest of ways.

The conclusion to be drawn from these considerations, even if the last argument is discounted, is that in the light of contemporary physics the human being cannot be regarded as consisting exclusively of physical parts 'whose law-governed interaction determines the behaviour of the system as a whole', which was how we expressed what amounted to our *second* conception of man as a machine. Physics itself tells us, without our listening to the less respectable voices of the vitalists or theologians or metaphysicians, that the behaviour of *no* physical system is rigorously determined: always and in principle there is an element of unpredictability.

5 *Materialism*

A straightforward response to this argument gives us a third conception of 'mechanism'. All reference to 'rigorously determined behaviour' is left out, and the claim is simply made that man is composed exclusively of the kind of things studied by physics: electrons, neutrons, protons and their 'components'. Then the modern mechanist would be understood as saying not that man is an unconscious robot, which would be absurd, nor that man's behaviour is rigorously determined by physical laws, which according to orthodox physics would be false, but that man is a highly organized lump of ordinary matter and *nothing more*. The features in man that we find, or have found in the past, so remarkable would on this view not call for the postulation of a special, uniquely human component (either physical or non-physical) in man's make-up, but would be explicable in terms of a specially high degree of organization of the ordinary physical matter with which physics is familiar. We need postulate no 'soul', that is to say, nor 'spirit', nor 'entelechy' to account for what we know of human beings. Man is not made up of the sort of matter with which physics deals *plus* a different kind of 'matter' — a 'spiritual substance', for example: he is made up of ordinary physical matter *only*, but of ordinary physical matter organized in a uniquely complex way. That, I suggest, is a third interpretation of what modern mechanists may be saying (and to my mind, as will be obvious, the interpretation that needs to be taken most seriously).

To evaluate it, however, we shall have to look carefully at those features of human beings which are often alleged to present most difficulties from this point of view. In a later section we shall consider others, but first we must recognize the difficulty that seems to many the most recalcitrant: human beings' *consciousness*.

3 Consciousness

1 *Introduction*

Many people have taken the view that any 'mechanical' or 'material-ist' conception of man is ruled out of court by the phenomenon of consciousness, and consequently that any attempt to study human beings based on this conception is basically misfounded. Human beings and perhaps some other animals, for that matter, not only behave in certain ways; they are *aware* of so behaving. They not only react to certain stimuli, they are (often) *aware* of what their sense organs tell them. They not only extricate themselves from situations that are harming their bodies, they *feel* pain. They not only exhibit 'goal-directed' behaviour, they consciously entertain and pursue purposes. Purely physical complexes, it is said, could never become 'aware' or 'conscious' in these ways. We may perhaps imagine computers being developed to a much more sophisticated degree than has been achieved so far, such that they would be capable of *doing* whatever the human being can *do*, and yet consciousness, it is said, would be necessarily lacking.

Our conscious experience, to put it another way, is intrinsically 'non-physical'. My toothache has no shape, no mass, no solidity. It doesn't make sense to ask how many centimetres long it is, nor to speak of it travelling through space. In all these respects it contrasts with a physical thing such as a nerve fibre or tooth.

We must admit then, it is argued, that there take place in the human being 'processes' other than physical ones — the thoughts, feelings, sensations, and so on, which make up the person's con-scious experience.

This line of thought continues with the idea that you can't have a *process* without a substance that *undergoes* the process. In the case of the physical processes connected with the human being there is the physical substance of which the body is made; in the case of the non-physical processes which have just been argued for, there must be a non-physical substance. It is this non-physical substance which comprises what we call a human being's *mind*.

2 *Dualism*

Some arrive at the view, therefore, that there is more to the human being than the physical matter of which his body is composed; there is also his mind, made up of non-physical 'matter'. The human being is an amalgam of two substances, physical and non-physical; a complex of two things, body and mind. A person thus 'lives through two collateral histories, one consisting of what happens in and to his body, the other consisting of what happens in and to his mind. ... The events in the first history are events in the physical world, those in the second are events in the mental world.'

These are the words of Gilbert Ryle, describing the conception that he proceeds to attack. His figure for the conception is striking. It is, he suggests, like thinking of a man as a *machine*, haunted by a *ghost*. He calls it, because he wants to reject it, a *myth*: Descartes's myth, the dogma of the ghost in the machine. It is less polemically known as *dualism*. Dualism has seemed absolutely inescapable to many people; but it leads to at least two stultifying abstract problems, and to one of a more practical nature.

2.1 *The body-mind relationship.*   The first is that of explaining the relationship between the two components of which man is supposed to be composed. The connection certainly seems to be intimate: my body collides with the table and I immediately 'feel' the contact, and perhaps a little pain; I decide to go for some coffee and my body immediately moves down to the kitchen. The 'collateral histories' of which Ryle speaks are thus closely interwoven, apparently interacting with each other over and over again.

But how can such contact take place? By accepting the non-physical nature of mental happenings, have we not ruled out the possibility of their having any effect on the physical, or of the physical on them? Descartes considered that the mind articulated with the body within a particular organ, and he was prepared to identify the pineal gland as the organ in question. People have tended to scoff at this suggestion, yet if the contact is to take place at all it must take place, one might think, *somewhere*, so that if we reject the hypothesis of the pineal gland we shall have to think of some different locus, which is likely to sound equally bizarre. For what is odd is not the particular idea that contact between physical and non-physical should take place at the pineal gland but rather the idea of physical and non-physical making *contact* at all.

The view that grasps this nettle fully is rewarded with the title of interactionism. Somehow there is contact, and the causal influence operates both ways. Mind affects body and body affects mind.

Less bold in this sense is *epiphenomenalism* which only manages to believe in one-way causal influence. The body affects the mind, but not vice-versa, so that we have the picture of mental phenomena 'thrown off' by the workings of the brain. Consciousness is seen as a kind of by-product of physical processes, a kind of gaseous effluent hovering over the factory below. On this view, the impression we have of our decisions sometimes affecting our bodily behaviour is an illusion.

A third view thinks that the impression we have of causal influence operating in that way — of bodily changes affecting the mind — is an illusion too. On this view, therefore, I have a body and I have a mind; but despite all appearances the two never interact. There *are* plenty of 'appearances' of interaction none the less, as we have already noted: for example, when sugar dissolves in my mouth I have a sweet taste; when I think of some acutely embarrassing past experience, I blush. How can these 'apparent' interactions be accounted for if no *real* interaction takes place? Perhaps there is no answer to this question that would satisfy modern ears, but one suggestion in the past has been that it is the Almighty who causes the appropriate mental event to accompany the bodily event that we think of as corresponding to it.

The first major problem that the dualist conception presents, therefore, is that of explaining how body and mind relate to each other. Second, it seems to imply that any particular person cannot really be sure that people other than himself have minds at all!

2.2 *Other minds.*   This is a difficulty that arises out of the 'privacy' that dualists regard as characterizing mental affairs. We can observe a man's body and its movements, the dualist says, but not what goes on in his mind. What goes on there seems to be a matter that is private to him. His overt behaviour is carried out 'on stage' for all to see; his thoughts, feelings, sensations, and so on, occur 'behind the scenes'.

It is this 'hiddenness' that allows us to raise the astounding question of *whether they are really there at all* — as far as other people are concerned, that is. I know that I myself have thoughts, feelings, sensations, and so on; that is, I know *I* have 'inner experience', a life of consciousness. But can I be sure the same is true of other people? I can never actually *see* their 'consciousness', it seems. All I see (or otherwise 'sense') are the movements another person's body engages in, including the movements of his vocal apparatus resulting in apparently intelligible speech. Maybe, it is suggested, there is no conscious mind behind these movements. Maybe the other person is what Descartes insisted he himself could not be, an unconscious robot.

2.2.1 *The argument from analogy.* A tempting response to this bizarre suggestion brings further into the open the conception of the mind we are dealing with. Mental events, it is said, are not *entirely* hidden from view. As far as I am concerned there is one person whose mental activity is perfectly accessible and observable: that is to say, *myself*. If we speak of mental phenomena occurring 'behind the scenes', therefore, we must agree that *to the person himself* his own thoughts, feelings, sensations, and so on, are perfectly accessible and observable.

From that initial claim, the argument proceeds to suggest that the things occurring in the mind are not perhaps as 'secretive' as we have so far been suggesting. Suppose, for example, I suddenly develop a severe pain in my throat, which is exacerbated every time I say anything. This inner, behind-the-scenes phenomenon will be signalled, surely, in my outward observable behaviour. I shall crease my brow, perhaps shut my eyes. I may drink a glass of water; or, if it got very bad, clutch my throat and collapse moaning to the floor. My pain, in other words, would register in my observable behaviour.

The same would be true, it is said, of many of my internal feelings, attitudes, and so on. If I felt miserable, it would show in the way I behaved. If I had a prejudice against people with big noses, my behaviour would show it. If I got very angry, the way I behaved would be modified, normally speaking, in a particular way.

Now, in my own case, I know what internal mental phenomena go with what distinctive pieces of overt behaviour. I know, for example, that scratching my forehead accompanies the internal feeling of puzzlement; I know that moaning and clutching at my throat is a sign of my internal feelings of pain in the throat; I know that cursing people with long noses, and reviling them, and knocking such a person down when one comes across one — I know that these are the overt actions that signify an inner feeling of hatred for the long-nosed.

But, the argument goes on, other people sometimes adopt behaviour which is similar to my behaviour when I am having internal experience of the sort indicated. Cannot I then argue by analogy and infer from their behaviour that they are having inner experience and, indeed, that they are having inner experience of a particular sort? For example: I notice that when I am feeling bored, I tend to shift about in my seat and fidget with my papers, and so on. Surely, when I see someone else going in for this distinctive kind of behaviour, I can infer that he too must be feeling bored?

Though mental phenomena are themselves unobservable, it is thus said, they are associated with bodily behaviour that *is* observable. In our own case we can both observe our own behaviour *and* peer behind the scenes to see what piece of behaviour is associated with what 'mental phenomenon'. And this enables us, simply by observing their behaviour, to tell not only that other people have minds but also what is going on in them.

This argument for the existence of other minds, which accepts and works within the dualist conception, is a tempting refuge for the dualist. But it suffers, many think, from one appalling weakness (and some say several). What we have to think about, the critic urges, is the basis on which it is established that an internal experience of a particular kind is associated with overt behaviour of a certain sort.

For example, we can ask on what do I base my assertion that putting my hand to my throat and moaning is associated with having the 'internal experience' of having a pain in my throat? The answer must be — since only my *own* inner experiences are accessible to me on the view we are considering — that I am basing my assertions of association on my own case alone. I see in my own case that moaning goes with internally feeling pain, and then assert quite generally that in *everybody's* case moaning goes with the internal feeling of pain. But, goes the criticism, surely this is an utterly unwarranted extrapolation? What possible right can I have to generalize from a *single* case to literally millions of cases? Here I am seeing that in one case, my own, a particular type of conscious experience is associated with a particular type of bodily behaviour, and then blandly assuming that the same association is there in everybody else's case. But why shouldn't *my* case be peculiar? Why shouldn't it be odd or idiosyncratic? On the view we are considering, it may be argued, *we could never know whether it was or not.*

So fails the strongest argument that dualism can muster for 'the existence of other minds' — such is a common opinion. In another instance, therefore, dualism gives rise to an intractable problem, and we have another reason for seeking an alternative.

2.3 *Introspectionism.* Moreover, when the dualist notion of the inaccessible 'privacy' of conscious experience is relied on as the starting point for psychology, vexing problems are at once generated. For in trying to engage in systematic study of the 'mind' psychology will then see itself as excluded from any *direct* observations of its subject matter. The psychologist will be able to observe the 'mind' directly only in his own case; for the rest, he can perform no direct observations at all, but must rely on people's *reports*. Psychology would then have to devote itself to asking its subjects to describe the contents of their conscious experiences — to 'look into' themselves, as it were, and describe precisely what they see. These descriptions would then constitute the data on which psychology would have to base itself.

Introspectionism was the name of the school that actually adopted these tenets, and it flourished in the early part of this century. The general difficulty it encountered springs directly from its 'dualist' character: its basic data were in an important sense 'uncheckable'. For how can one confirm or disconfirm a report of a conscious experience? If one's subject is asked to describe what he 'sees' at a given moment and he reports that he sees a square patch of blue, you have to take his word for it. You can't take the top off his mind and check whether he is reporting correctly or not. Nor can you check by asking him to check *himself*, to 'look' again most carefully at the experience he has described and say exactly what he 'sees': because then he will be describing the experience he is having at a time *later* than the time at which he had the experience he was originally asked to report on. That is, he will be describing in his 'checking' report a different experience from the one he originally tried to describe. One can, in other words, introspect one's *present* experience only *once*.

An exponent of introspectionism cannot therefore claim that his data are checkable on the grounds that the subject himself can have a second and closer look; and it is even more obvious that there is no possibility of anybody other than the subject being called in. If we want to check up on the 'content' of a particular person's consciousness, the testimony of another party will be of no relevance at all.

It may be asked, however, why it is so vital that one's basic data should be checkable, and in this connection we may quickly refer to the fact that a general philosophical thesis of great influence in recent decades maintains that the whole significance of what we say depends on its checkability, so that a statement which could not in principle be checked must be regarded as simply lacking content, or senseless. This general principle aside, however, the uncheckability of introspectionism's basic data generated more straightforward difficulty when different workers within the school began to produce conflicting results. It meant that nothing could be done to settle the conflicts one way or another, so that psychology began to look hardly like a proper science at all. Many of its practitioners embraced with relief, therefore, the new methodology that rejected (at least for practical purposes) the dualism upon which introspectionism was based and turned instead, as we do now, to a 'behaviourist' conception of human beings' 'mentality'.

3 *Logical behaviourism*

Taking its cue partly from the difficulties encountered by dualism in accepting the existence of 'other minds', the approach that has come to be called 'logical behaviourism' defends the remarkable idea that our stress on 'conscious experience', on 'awareness', is entirely misplaced, because there is *no such thing*. We are invited to ponder the fact that in our ordinary talk we are perfectly prepared to speak of other people as thinking this and that, as 'feeling' discomfort or pleasure, as 'suffering' from jealousy, as 'planning' to do such and such. We are quite prepared to apply to others 'mental' words (or, in the jargon, mental *predicates*). Yet, as our exposition of the problem of other minds brought out, our only basis for knowing whether we are applying those words correctly is the *observable behaviour* of the person concerned; so that if the words in fact refer to mental occurrences taking place behind the scenes, as the dualist holds, we could never know whether we were really justified in applying them to other people or not, and therefore there would be no sense in applying these words at all.

The logical behaviourist's conclusion is that mental words do *not* in fact refer to mental occurrences behind the scenes: they refer to *aspects of a person's behaviour*. When we say that a man is angry, according to this view, we are not describing an internal mental experience; we are saying how the man is behaving or likely to behave. We are saying that he is liable to shout, and shout unreasonably harsh things, try to injure whatever has angered him, reject requests he might at other times have met, and so on. If we say that so-and-so feels unwell, we mean not that he is undergoing a certain kind of secret inner experience, but that he is likely to turn pale, lie down, take an aspirin, consult the doctor, and so on.

Having outlined this doctrine I have to say that it is very difficult to find anyone actually defending it! The philosopher Gilbert Ryle comes nearest to doing so, but in the course of his arguments on the topic (to be found in his very influential book *The Concept of Mind*) he refers to 'neat sensation words' in such a way as to suggest that even he does not embrace the doctrine wholeheartedly. Nevertheless his understanding of *motives* would represent an example of what I am calling the 'logical behaviourist' approach.

3.1 *Ryle's analysis of 'motive'.* According to the 'two-worlds' view, a motive, says Ryle, refers to an internal mental event preceding the external physical action of which it is the motive. If we say that the motive of someone's boasting was vanity, we shall be construed, on the two-worlds view, as asserting that the boasting was preceded by a mentally experienced impulse of vanity which caused the piece of boasting concerned. So to construe motive explanations is to regard them as analogous to the type of explanation exemplified by 'the window broke because a stone hit it'.

In criticizing this view of motives, Ryle points out that there is another kind of explanation which could quite properly be given in the case of the broken window: we may say that the glass broke because *it was brittle*. Now we are not referring to an event, but rather to a characteristic of the glass. We are describing what tends to happen to glass when it is struck. This provides us with a better understanding of motive explanations, argues Ryle. For, in terms of our example, in saying that a man boasted out of vanity we are saying not that an 'impulse' of vanity resulted in his boasting, but that his boasting fits into a general pattern of vain behaviour. To say that a man is vain is parallel to saying that a piece of glass is brittle: the glass tends to fragment when struck, the man tends to do what he can to attract 'the admiration and envy of others' when given the opportunity. In saying that the boaster's motive was vanity, therefore, we are invoking not a preoccurring mental impulse, as the two-words view would maintain, but a pattern of behaviour; and a similar account can be given, according to Ryle, of ascriptions of motives in other cases.

This is not the whole of Ryle's account of motives, nor, of course, is it the whole of his account of mental concepts. But it illustrates the kind of understanding that logical behaviourism wishes to substitute for the two-worlds view.

It is a conception that we could understand being very attractive to a scientifically minded person who wished to study the human being. On a two-worlds view a good deal of what is important to the human being is rather mysterious and very difficult of access. The student is easily lured into introspectionism with all its methodological embarrassments. A logical-behaviourist view, on the other hand, implies that, although the human being may be complicated, he is *altogether observable*: in studying what he does we are studying all there is to him.

3.2 *Objections to logical behaviourism.*   But its attractiveness cannot be allowed to obscure what may be regarded as its glaring and hopeless defect: the denial of what we have been calling the 'conscious experience' of human beings. *Having a pain* is surely more than having a tendency to go in for a certain sort of behaviour: it is something *felt*. In denying that a man in pain actually experiences a sensation of pain the logical behaviourist is surely denying the undeniable.

Logical behaviourism holds, therefore, that in talking of a person's *mind*, and generally in applying mental words to him, we are simply talking about his behaviour. To study the human being's behaviour *is* to study his mind. Its weakness, one might think exasperatingly obvious and damning, is that it has to deny the reality of conscious experience.

3.3 *Psychological behaviourism.*   In *psychological behaviourism* a way is found of adopting what is attractive in the logical version without these extreme and generally unacceptable implications. Though it is a moot point whether the founding father of psychological behaviourism, J. B. Watson, actually denied the reality of conscious experience, his followers have certainly not generally wished to do so. What they have argued is that psychology may and must *ignore* conscious experience if it is to establish anything worthwhile. Including in psychological data uncheckable descriptions of people's states of consciousness introduces all the 'subjectivity' which made introspectionism less than a science. Progress in the scientific understanding of the human being can only come with the study of objective matters — in particular of the environment as it affects the individual through his senses, and of the individual's publicly observable responses thereto. Psychological behaviourism thus devotes itself, as Broadbent puts it, to relating 'events at the bodily senses ("stimuli") to events at those parts of the body which act on the outer world ("responses")'.

4   *The 'identity' hypothesis*

The second major alternative to dualism concedes, in a sense, that besides the reality of physical events in the body (and particularly in the brain) there is the reality of conscious experience: yet it proposes that these realities are one and the same. A conscious experience, for example a pain I have, is to be regarded as *being* a particular neuro-physiological event or sequence of events in my brain. It is vital to see that this suggestion is not simply that each conscious experience has a pattern of brain activity associated with it (which would be a dualist view). It is that the conscious experience just *is* a particular pattern of events in the brain.

One way (which can be very dangerously misleading) of expressing this idea is to say that there is *one* thing that looks differently from two points of view. A neuro-surgeon looks at a patient's brain and sees it from the outside as a physical object, and perhaps, indirectly, he observes some of the processes within it. But the patient himself, whose brain it is, has an inside view of the brain, as it were, and it is this inside view which constitutes his conscious experience. The same physical process which the neuro-surgeon observes from outside constitutes for the insider his conscious thought. As the lightning is to the discharge, so a man's sensation of pain, for example, is to a certain pattern of events in the brain.

The difficulty with such a view is as striking as in the case of logical behaviourism. How can it be asserted that a certain brain process *is* a conscious experience? Isn't the idea simply a contradiction in terms? What we mean by a 'conscious experience', it is thus suggested, simply rules out its being *one and the same thing* as a physical process. It may be argued, for example, that if I were to daydream about a forthcoming holiday it would not make sense to ask *exactly where in the brain* my *thoughts* were (it is partly the fact that it seems inappropriate to locate conscious experiences spatially that leads us to say they are not physical). But a particular event or sequence of events in the brain *can* be located precisely. How then can the daydream and the brain event(s) be one and the same?

5 *Concluding remarks*

What light do these considerations throw on the problem that prompted them — the question of whether the phenomena of the mind rule out a mechanical conception of man? They bring to the fore, at any rate, the fact that non-dualist theories of the mind have been seriously put forward. Both logical behaviourism and the identity theory seem at least compatible with the final 'mechanist' conception we distinguished earlier — the conception that denies that there is more to the human being than the elementary physical particles of which his body is composed.

After pursuing the arguments just outlined here, however, one may well conclude that the objections to both these major rivals of dualism are so obvious and so destructive as to make one wonder how anyone could seriously embrace either. But then, again after due consideration of the arguments, one may well conclude that the deficiencies of dualism itself are equally damning. The problem of the nature of the mind or the mental side of the human being is indeed a persistent and intractable problem just because there is reason to think that *all* the alternative 'solutions' are untenable.

4 Man as an animal

1 *Introduction*

In the same way that there have been claims that man is 'just a machine', others have argued that the proper methodological attitude is to regard man as an *animal*. The zoologist Desmond Morris puts this across very succinctly in the title of one of his several stimulating and widely read books *The Naked Ape*. The dust-jacket goes on to explain:

> In *The Naked Ape* an eminent zoologist puts man firmly in his place — alongside the one hundred and ninety two other species of apes and monkeys, among which he is most easily distinguished by the nakedness of his skin … Man remains — despite his erudition and inspirations — essentially a primate. Whether in his sexual or social life, in his aggressions or affections, in his eating habits or religious beliefs, he still follows the fundamental patterns of behaviour set down by his hunting ape ancestors.

Morris himself declares — and the quotation is representative of his style — '[The] unusual and highly successful species (*Homo sapiens*) spends a great deal of time examining his higher motives and an equal amount of time studiously ignoring his fundamental ones. He is proud that he has the biggest brain of all the primates, but attempts to conceal the fact that he also has the biggest penis.'

If we are to understand man's behaviour, goes this thesis, we must look at him as an animal. We shall be able to understand the nature of war, for example, if we remember what is known about the functions of fighting among animals — which is the particular argument of another widely read book in this field, Konrad Lorenz's *On Aggression*.

For the sake of a label, let us call the view we are discussing the 'ethological' view of man. It is the view that the study of man's behaviour is a branch of the study of animal behaviour: that the social sciences, I suppose one could say, are part of ethology. In asking about its validity we are asking about the differences between man and the (rest of the) animal kingdom: are they so great that the methods of study and way of understanding appropriate to the one are inappropriate to the other?

2   *Physical autonomy*

One difference that might occur to someone thinking along biological lines is the degree to which man is physically independent of his natural environment.

To understand the force of this suggestion we have to bear in mind the general working of evolution. Take any naturally occurring group of animals sharing the same lifestyle. The built-in programme according to which an animal develops — that is, its genetic apparatus — ensures that each member of the group is slightly different from all the others. That is to say, the group will show 'variation'. But this means that some animals are likely to be better adapted than others to the physical conditions around them. For example, the gazelle with slightly stronger leg muscles will be better able to escape its attackers. Because its style of life involves being preyed upon by carnivores, that is to say, improved leg muscles will increase its adaptation to its environment. Now, those animals which are better adapted are more likely to survive to sexual maturity than are their less well-adapted brethren; and since their offspring will inherit their strong legs, the proportion of strong-legged gazelles will increase with the next generation. The net result is increasing adaptation to the environment by the group of animals as a whole. Each generation is just a little bit better adapted than its predecessor.

What we have sketched here is, of course, the core of the Darwinian theory of evolution by natural selection. One formulation would be that populations of organisms show progressive adaptation to their environment as a result of natural selection acting on genetically controlled variation.

In certain circumstances, when competition becomes intense, certain individuals are able to move out of their original environment and colonize a new one which they then proceed to exploit.

This is what happened, for example, when the animal kingdom, hitherto restricted entirely to an environment of water, expanded on to the land, which presented new and tremendous possibilities of food and lifestyle to animals used to the strictly limited food supply and consequently harsh competition of the overpopulated seas and rivers. New environments are thus explored whenever the opportunity presents itself; and the process of adaptation to the different conditions that newly prevail receives a fresh impetus.

Another factor is that environments themselves change, and animals once perfectly adapted to them have to *re*adapt to the altered conditions, or else perish. Sometimes, in adapting to an environment, an organism loses its flexibility, as it were, and in the event of its environment changing it finds it has lost the power to keep pace: it swiftly becomes extinct. As is well known, this may have been the fate of the dinosaur and his bulky friends. Having devoted infinite pains to accommodating their large persons to the demands and exigencies of life in the swamp, they woke up one morning to find the plug out, as it were, and the water going down fast. But it was too late to do anything. They were so committed, biologically, to swamp life, that they had lost the ability to *re*adapt, and were quickly eliminated.

The sea-urchins represent the opposite possibility. They adapted to their environment millions of years ago, and have remained virtually unchanged ever since. This is simply a consequence of the fact that during this immense period their environment — the bottom of the sea — has remained unaltered, so that these comfortable little creatures have simply been able to stay as they were.

Organisms are thus able to adapt progressively to external conditions, to readapt to changing conditions and to exploit new environments. But some organisms go even further and by a final sophistication evolve in the direction of freeing themselves totally of their environments.

One of the mechanisms working towards this end is that which keeps our internal body temperature constant. The temperature outside our bodies varies considerably, as we are well aware, but by bringing into play such mechanisms as shivering, sweating, and adjusting the bore of our surface blood vessels we contrive to keep our internal temperature remarkably constant, so much so that a variation of less than five degrees has us flat on our backs with a doctor in anxious attendance. But this only occurs when the mechanisms have broken down. Normally they secure the independence of our internal temperature effectively enough.

Where we score over the other warmblooded animals, however, is in the supra-biological mechanisms we have invented to secure and extend our independence. What human beings have done is to *build* an environment to suit themselves, instead of adapting themselves to an external environment that is indifferent to their purposes and needs. You see an extreme form of this in the human being's first steps into space — an unsympathetic environment, indeed, with its extremes of heat and cold, its airlessness, the lack of gravity, bombardment by meteorites and radiation. But space-travellers build round themselves an artificial shell which supplies their biological needs and protects them from the inhospitable elements outside.

In our everyday lives, however, the degree of our emancipation from the baneful influence of our natural environment is almost as obvious. We have central heating and air conditioning; we wear clothes, have electric lighting, store water, know how to preserve and even synthesize food, have come near to conquering disease, threaten even to combat the process of ageing itself. We can govern our climate by going indoors, and we are not far from being able to govern it out of doors too. We walk on tarmac and dispose of our sewage along sanitary pipes. For the rich world's very poor, in the large American city slums, for example, life can be lived out in its entirety in the kind of concrete desert depicted so well in *West Side Story*, while for the very rich any contact with nature unstructured by man may be just as tenuous, as they fly from one Hilton to the next and get their only breath of fresh air as they step from aircraft to airport coach.

In these respects it seems true that man to a remarkable degree has become independent of his natural environment, and clear that he is hardly rivalled in this sense by any other representative of the animal kingdom. But is this distinction, as we have so far developed it, significant methodologically? Does it necessitate an approach to the study of man which is different from that appropriate in the case of (other) animals?

I think the answer at this stage of the discussion is probably No. But there are subtler aspects of the human being's allegedly unique autonomy to be considered. The most profound aspect of their emancipation, it may be claimed, is a product of their unique capacity to *learn*. In pursuing this idea, as I do now, I shall be considering a number of more specific claims that have been made about man's uniqueness.

3   *Instinctive and learnt behaviour*

We have already seen how the theory of natural selection enables us to understand the development of *structures* that promote an individual organism's chance of survival. Now we have to note that *patterns of behaviour* can be thought of as developing in the same way.

It is possible to isolate in the case of many animals certain patterns of behaviour that seem to be genetically controlled: present the individual with certain stimuli and the patterns will be elicited, irrespective of any previous experience the individual may have had. The begging behaviour of herring-gull chicks is usually claimed to be an example. The appearance of the parent's beak, particularly with its red spot, over the side of the nest triggers a pecking action on the part of the chicks (and this in turn induces the parent to regurgitate what then serves as the chick's meal). This pecking action, it is claimed, does not have to be learnt. Mutations in the genes controlling such behaviour patterns might improve the contribution of the behaviour to the individual's chances of survival, and so as generations passed would tend to spread throughout the population. Thus we can understand how behaviour that was well adapted to a population's environment would tend to become established.

Behaviour patterns that are genetically determined in the way just described I shall call *instinctive*, so that with this use of terms, which is widely if not universally accepted, instinctive behaviour is behaviour whose pattern is determined, as it were, by innate mechanisms *within* the animal: the role of the environment is merely to throw a switch which brings a preorganized sequence of movements into play. The life of the insects, for example, displays this kind of behaviour in a very highly developed form.

With the refinement of the brain during the course of evolution there arises, however, a new kind of relationship between organisms and environment. Instinctive patterns of behaviour are, as I have said, triggered by particular features in the animal's surroundings and consequently, where an animal lives by behaviour of this type, its apprehension of its surroundings need only be relatively unsophisticated. The creature must be able to sense the appropriate 'trigger-stimuli' but does not need to build up any general picture of the environment as it is from moment to moment.

Instinctive behaviour, however, has severe limitations. Should the environment to which it is adapted *change*, to take the most important case, the animal's behaviour may become completely inappropriate. A particular species of vole may have been preyed on for an evolutionarily significant time by, say, the buzzard, and its instinctive escape reaction may have become tied to the 'trigger-stimulus' of a brown shape circling above. Should a *new* predator, lacking the distinctive spiralling flight pattern of the buzzard, come to develop an interest in the vole, the latter might find itself wiped out unless evolutionary processes worked quickly enough to establish a new trigger-link between the escape reaction and the new threat.

Learning, in its varying degrees of sophistication, is the evolutionary response to this situation. Mechanisms are developed which enable the organism to learn during the course of its own lifetime how to respond most appropriately to its situation. This involves in the first place a widening of the extent to which the organism is aware of its surroundings. Sensing trigger-stimuli are no longer sufficient: what is necessary, if flexibility of response is to develop, is that somehow the creature should be aware of the state of its surroundings as a whole. Means have to evolve whereby an organism forms some kind of representation of its surroundings 'in its mind'.

As creatures who share this sophistication we can readily appreciate the point being made. My awareness, for example, is not limited to trigger-stimuli — particular colours, shapes, sounds, smells. I have, rather, an all-round picture of my surroundings: I see through my window to the back garden and to the backs of houses beyond, and see buckets and flowers and a cat playing havoc with the rockery. These items, we ordinarily think at any rate, are out there in the world quite independent of me. But I am aware of them. They figure in the internal representation I have of my surroundings.

Being able to form such an internal representation is, then, the first requirement if instinctive behaviour patterns are to be replaced by behaviour that is learnt. The second is that of learning itself: the animal must be able to discover how to respond effectively to the situation as it appreciates it. There is no point in a thirsty animal which has abandoned instinctive behaviour 'knowing' that there is a pool of water in front of it unless it also 'knows' how to drink from it.

It is often claimed that the distinction we now have in outline before us between *instinctive* and *learnt* behaviour is deeply significant for any attempt to identify the distinctiveness of the human being. True, it could not seriously be maintained that learning is restricted to human beings. But learnt behaviour, it is often said, *does* play a uniquely important role in our life, with instincts being abandoned almost entirely.

This is a suggestion to bear in mind perhaps as we go on now to distinguish different types of learning. It might be that what is distinctive about man is not so much that he relies on learning as opposed to instinct but that his learning is of a special type.

4 *Trial-and-error and 'insight'*

The first means of discovering what is an appropriate response to a
situation as an animal perceives it has been labelled learning by
'trial-and-error'. The creature simply engages in behaviour 'at
random' until it hits on something that does the trick. Chicks, for
example, appear to hatch without the instinctive knowledge of how
to drink. What they can be observed to do is to go about pecking at
whatever they come across, in an apparently unguided manner.
When they happen to peck at the surface of some water — held in a
pan, say — they nevertheless 'accidentally' get a drink. Thus is
solved the problem of acquiring water on that particular occasion —
and also, because the chick is able to *learn* from the experience, the
problem of how to drink in general.

Many animals exhibit learning by trial-and-error, and no doubt
human beings do too. But human beings also display learning that is
manifestly not of this type, it may be said. Faced with a situation
they have not encountered before, human beings are capable (at
times) of discovering the appropriate response *without* any apparent
recourse to trial-and-error. A space engineer doesn't have to fire a
long series of rockets in random directions in order to discover the
right aim for the moon. A father doesn't have to make experiments
in order to take his child's plastic train to pieces; and if it's a very
simple puzzle or a very old child, nor does the child.

All these cases could be said to involve 'reasoning'. Instead of trying possibilities at random the father, and perhaps his child, *works
out* how the parts fit together; the engineer calculates, on the basis of
accepted scientific theory, the launch angle of the moon shot. And it
is, of course, a familiar suggestion that it is precisely this ability to
think out solutions to problems — the ability to 'reason' — that is the
distinctive feature of man.

Leaving the delicate notion of 'reason' on one side for a moment,
let us take note of a related concept that animal psychologists sometimes invoke. The human case of solving problems by 'thought'
rather than by trial-and-error is paralleled, it is claimed, in certain
animals, which can be observed, on occasion, simply to pause in the
face of a new situation and then go straight to a solution.

In a famous series of observations on chimpanzees, Wolfgang
Köhler explored the problem-solving ability of non-human primates,
and reported some incidents that have been interpreted in this way.
Köhler would set an animal a problem, like leaving a banana in sight
but out of reach of a hungry chimpanzee, and watch to see if and
how it arrived at a solution. The use of a stick to draw the food

closer seemed easily discovered, and in some cases, where two sticks were provided but neither long enough to reach the food on their own, the observed animal fitted the sticks together to form a tool that *was* long enough for the job.

Mostly, the animals' solutions seemed to be based on playing around with the situation until success was hit upon accidentally — the process, in other words, seemed to be one of trial-and-error. But in at least one case, Köhler seems to report — I say 'seems' because what he says is ambiguous — an animal reacted to a new situation not by engaging in random 'experimentation' but by sitting down, pausing and then proceeding straight to a successful response.

A more developed example of animal problem-solving which does not seem to involve trial-and-error — and which has been put for that reason under the perhaps unfortunate heading of 'insightful' behaviour — is provided by an experiment with rats by E. C. Tolman and C.H. Honzik. Using a raised set of pathways as shown in Figure 1, these workers first subjected a rat to a preliminary training session

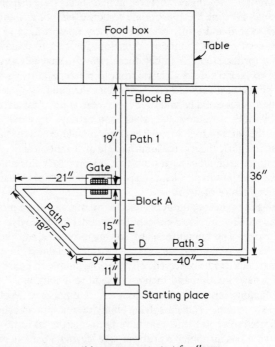

Fig 1 *Tolman and Honzik's apparatus to test for 'learning by insight' in the rat*
(After Tolman and Honzik, 'Insight in Rats')

during which it learnt that whenever Path 1 is blocked at Block A the food box can be reached by either of Paths 2 or 3. The block is then moved from A to B. The rat is released and, should it proceed down Path 1, it discovers the block at the new location. The question is, then, when it has returned to the main junction, which path it will choose next. Path 2 will lead it to the block again; but Path 3 gives access to the food. These considerations will, however, be inaccessible to the rat, if its problem-solving is indeed limited to trial-and-error. One would in that case expect the creature to be equally likely to choose 2 or 3. In a long series of experiments with different rats one would thus expect, on this hypothesis, the number of experiments in which the rat chose Path 2 at this juncture to be roughly equal to the number of experiments in which the rat chose Path 3. The result reported, however, was that in a statistically significant larger proportion of experiments, the rat chose Path 3.

What this shows, it is claimed, is that the rat employs 'insight' in such situations. Faced with the new situation of encountering a block at B, the animal must be somehow 'working out' on the basis of its previous experiences with the run that Path 2 will be as useless as Path 1, and that Path 3 is the best choice.

The development of insight learning seems a striking departure from the method of trial-and-error. It has been suggested, however, that the difference is not as radical as it seems. Perhaps, it has been suggested, 'insight' represents trial-and-error that has been *internalized*. In terms of our example, perhaps what the rat with 'insight' is doing is conducting a 'thought experiment' in the place of an actual one. Having discovered the block at B and returned to the major junction, instead of *physically* trying Path 2 it *imagines* itself doing so — only to discover, in its imagination, the path blocked. Then, it is suggested, it *imagines* itself running along Path 3 and finding access to the food at the end. Its actual choice of path is then made in the light of these imaginings.

The process of *thinking* that seems to be involved when a rat makes the rational choice is conceived of on this approach as a kind of mental substitute for physical action. As the psychologist O. L. Zangwill has put it, in connection with the example not of the rat but of the ape 'pondering' prior to arriving at a successful solution: 'one might suppose that the ape tries out various courses of action "mentally" before putting any of them into action'.

At this point we have to return to the difficult notion of 'reasoning' that we put on one side some time ago. For the conception of 'insight' and the explanation of it in terms of 'mentalizing' the physical process of trial-and-error has been applied not just in rat and chimpanzee studies, but to the thinking of our own species. Observing that the essential feature of thinking is that it mediates between 'stimulus' and 'response', C. T. Morgan in a well-known psychology text avers: 'When we are solving problems (mental) processes substitute for things we might otherwise do overtly in a trial-and-error manner.' Yet another attempt to identify man's uniqueness is thus threatened, for, as I pointed out earlier, it is exactly the ability to 'think out' the solutions to problems — the ability to 'reason' — that many have singled out as the speciality of the human being. Studies like those on the chimpanzee and on the rat provide evidence of animals engaging in mental trial-and-error, so it has been maintained, and if all thinking is of this kind then once again what had been claimed as peculiarly human has been shown to occur much more widely.

5 *Theorizing*

It has also been argued, however, and to my mind correctly, that there is more to human thinking than the idea of 'mental trial-and-error' allows.

A human being faced with the problem confronting the rat would surely be able to put to himself the following considerations: 'With the block at B the common exit of Paths 1 and 2 is closed. Since Path 3 has a different exit, that is the path to choose.' Are we forced to say that this process of theorizing is just another way of expressing the trial-and-error thought process, or does it represent something quite different?

It may well be thought that there *is* something different in the 'line of thought' I have sketched; for in contrast to mental trial-and-error it involves the problem-solver in bringing to bear *general principles*. As far as trial-and-error is concerned, physical or mental, an animal behaves at random until it hits upon success; but in the 'line of thought' just outlined, we are imagining a problem-solver bringing to bear the general principle that if one path is blocked in a passage which it has in common with another path, that path will also be blocked.

Can non-human animals be considered to bring general principles to bear on problems? Can they be thought of as 'theorizing' in this way? It has been argued that they cannot and that it is exactly this that makes all the difference between us and them: human animals can theorize and others cannot. The important thesis that I now want to explain is that this special ability to theorize springs from our *language*, which is alleged to be of a uniquely sophisticated kind.

5.1 *Non-human language.* A study of communication among non-human animals quickly suggests that language in a wide sense is not restricted to the human being. Whenever reproduction relies on the interaction of two individuals, for example, as it does with us and with many other animals, the activities of the two have to be synchronized. It's no good for one of them to do his bit, unless the other does hers. Communication is therefore necessary to bring the two into the appropriate relationship; and so we have at least one reason why species develop often very complicated pre-mating rituals, where a piece of behaviour in one individual triggers off a different piece of behaviour on the part of a second individual which in turn triggers off a further piece of behaviour on the part of the first, and so on. This series of reciprocal triggerings culminates in the sexual act itself, and it serves to keep each individual's development towards that point in step, as it were, so that they both reach it together.

Consider, for example, the mating behaviour of the three-spined stickleback, as described by the ethologist Niko Tinbergen. During the breeding season, the male stickleback builds a nest, turns brilliant red, and parades up and down his territory. Females, in schools, pass by from time to time, their bodies swollen with eggs. The male reacts to their presence by performing a 'zigzag dance', driving at a female, then turning away, then driving towards her again. If she is ready, the female reacts to this by turning to the male and standing almost on her tail. His response is to turn and swim to the nest. She follows. He then thrusts his snout into the entrance and lies sideways. This induces the female to wriggle into the nest. Now the male brings things to their climax by prodding the base of her tail with his snout, whereupon she spawns, and retires. The male then enters the nest, fertilizes the eggs, chases the female away, restores the roof of the nest and (often) adjusts the eggs. The mating ceremony is then complete.

We have an example here, it seems clear, of a complicated pattern of animal communication; and we might easily be tempted to say that the system of signs employed by the stickleback constitutes an elementary *language*.

Perhaps a more complicated language, and certainly one whose mystery was very elusive, is that used by honey-bees. A scout bee which has discovered a new source of pollen has to tell his colleagues on returning to the hive exactly where the new supply is to be found. From a great deal of study it is now clear that this knowledge is imparted by the performance of a kind of dance. Somehow, by performing the appropriate movements, the scout bee is able to tell the others how far to fly and in what direction. Here perhaps we have an even stronger temptation to say that an elementary — or perhaps not-so-elementary — language is in use.

5.2 *Human language.*   But why does this temptation arise? What is it about the bees' behaviour that makes us think of it as quasi-linguistic?

One suggestion is that the essential thing about a language is that patterns of behaviour on the part of a creature come to stand for things other than themselves — for states of affairs in the world in which the creature lives. Where a pattern of behaviour is part of a language, in other words, there are rules linking the behaviour to features of the world. The behaviour is symbolic: it *signifies*, it *means* something. It is thus the fact that the dance movements of the scout bee seem to stand for something, to represent a feature of the bee's environment (the location of the new pollen), that gives rise to the idea that they constitute a language.

The contemporary philosopher Jonathan Bennett, sympathetic to this general approach, goes on to claim in his monograph on *Rationality* that if we think of linguistic behaviour as behaviour that correlates with states of affairs in the creature's environment we can pinpoint the uniqueness of *human* language. The non-human animal, thinks Bennett, can only represent in its behaviour particular states of affairs that obtain in its current environment. The human being, on the other hand, can represent states of affairs that obtained in the past, and even states of affairs that are *general.*

What is meant by *past* states of affairs is perhaps clear: the existence of pollen in such-and-such a place would count as a current state of affairs, and the honey-bee 'language' seems capable of representing this; but the existence of pollen at such-and-such a place *this time last year* would be a state of affairs that obtained in the past, a state of affairs that Bennett (referring to the evidence) argues bee 'language' cannot represent.

An example of a *general* state of affairs would be the fact, if it were one, that 'pollen is usually found on purple flowers'. Bennett thinks that such states of affairs cannot be represented in bee 'language' either. For a general state of affairs is a number of particular states of affairs somehow brought together, and Bennett thinks that this 'bringing together' or *synthesis* is a capacity unique to human language.

Bennett's point can perhaps be put by saying that animal quasi-linguistic behaviour can always be regarded as nothing but direct responses to some particular feature of the creature's 'environment'.

Think of the mother rabbit warning her offspring of the approach of danger, which she does by beating the ground with her hind feet: another example, we might be tempted to say, of a primitive language being used. The beating of the hind feet can be interpreted as meaning: 'There is an enemy approaching.' The present point is that the rabbit's action can be understood as a direct response to a feature actually present in the environment, namely the scent of the approaching stoat, or whatever. Using the term with which we are already perhaps overfamiliar, we might say that smelling the scent simply *triggers* the response — the beating of the hind feet.

The claim is that studies of animal behaviour so far enable us to interpret their communication as in every case following the same basic pattern. It may show surface complications and seem more sophisticated, but in all cases, goes the claim, the fundamental pattern depends on 'reflex' response to presented particular stimuli.

It is not at all difficult to see the stickleback's behaviour as fitting this pattern, with each new move in the ritual being triggered by the one that preceded it. With the honey-bee, however, things are more complicated. According to this view, the dance is to be understood as a direct response to 'memory traces' in the nervous system. The presence of the pollen, the direction of the sun, and the strength and direction of the wind are, it is supposed, coded in the memory of the bee, and the particular form of dance performed by the creature on returning to the hive is triggered by these memory traces. If the dance is to be understood as a 'statement', goes the argument, the 'statement' must be understood as non-general, or 'particular', and present tense: 'There is pollen in direction X, Y flying minutes away.'

Consider, on the other hand, some of the statements (now without quotation marks) made by human beings. During the course of a lesson a teacher seeing someone turn round to look at the clock may pass the remark that so-and-so is getting bored. His statement would be a particular one about something in the present and could be construed (if all other evidence of human linguistic powers were ignored) as a simple response on the teacher's part to the visual impression of the person's looking at the clock. But if his remark instead were to the effect that people usually got bored, say, three-quarters of the way through a lesson he would be making a *general* statement which *could not be* construed on the same pattern. In saying that people usually get bored about this time, he is going beyond his present visual impressions, and going beyond any 'memory trace' he might have of past impressions: he is *synthesizing* a number of visual impressions, embracing them in a single *general* statement.

Notice that the visual impressions brought together in a general statement are not restricted to the present: they include past ones too. 'People usually get bored three-quarters of the way through a lesson' subsumes past experiences as well as the present one of seeing so-and-so look at the clock. Making a general statement thus involves the ability to make statements about the past.

Bennett's claim, then, is that human language confers the unique ability to represent past states of affairs, and to represent states of affairs that embrace a number of particular past and particular present states of affairs — that is, states of affairs that are *general*.

We are now in a position to return to the rat confronting the newly moved block. The question we raised was whether we could think of the rat as weighing the consideration that 'if one path is blocked in a passage which it has in common with another path, that path will also be blocked.' The approach we have been developing would return a clear No to this possibility. For such a consideration would be *general* in form, and it is precisely general judgements which, according to the present approach, are unique to the possessors of human-type language. Bringing to bear general principles is just what other creatures cannot do.

We have the suggestion before us, then, that what is special about human beings is that they can arrive at an appropriate response to the situation in which they find themselves by bringing to bear *general* judgements, which they are able to arrive at by an act of synthesis applied to *several* experiences they have had in the past. We have noted also two less sophisticated ways in which animals which have a general apprehension of their surroundings may arrive at the appropriate response: first, actual and second, internalized or 'imaginary', *trial-and-error*.

6 *Learning from others*

But there is yet another way in which an appropriate response may be discovered by the individual, and it is one which has been also argued to have a profound bearing on the nature of human life. The method is simply to capitalize on the fact that in many cases *other* individuals will have discovered an appropriate response already: the uninitiated may either simply imitate the cognoscenti, or they may get the latter, as it were, to *teach* them what to do.

Direct imitation of the successful behaviour of others seems to occur not at all widely as far as animals in general are concerned. The biologist W. H. Thorpe, an outstanding authority in the field of animal learning, asserts that absolutely clear evidence of it has been obtained only for certain primates, though others have thought observations on cats as convincing, and still others think that this type of learning, sometimes called 'imitative' or 'observational', occurs in chicks.

It may be, then, that in the process of learning by imitation we have something that *does* play a specially important role in the human species. But the other process I mentioned — the possibility of one individual being actively *taught* by another — is perhaps even more significant.

In the wild, one can easily conceive of teaching taking place: a youngster performs a certain piece of behaviour by accident — in the course of random exploratory behaviour, perhaps — which its parents then pick out for reward (or, less happily, they may pick it out as the only piece of behaviour that does not elicit punishment). But this type of learning has figured even more prominently in psychologists' experimental work. It was, for example, the principle of learning from teaching on which the classical experiments of the American psychologist E. L. Thorndike rested — and it also provided the foundation for the (in)famous development of Thorndike's method, the Skinner box.

In Thorndike's original work, a hungry cat was imprisoned within a cage fitted with a door which could be released by a downward pull on a loop of string. To obtain food, the cat had to learn the trick of pulling on the string. An inexperienced animal — inexperienced in the ingenuity of Thorndike, that is — would scratch about in the region of the door but make no direct effort to pull at the string. Eventually, by accident, the string would get pulled, and the cat escape through the doorway to its meal. Returned to the cage again and again under the same conditions, the cat would be quicker and quicker at getting out again, until in the end it would effect an exit by pulling the string, as Barnett puts it, 'with elegant economy of effort' the moment it was placed inside.

Here, then, we have one animal — in this case a human being — teaching another a piece of behaviour by bringing to bear a combination of punishment and reward (string pulling is rewarded by food, other elements of the cat's random behaviour are punished in a sense by growing hunger).

Although many species of animals can be taught by *human beings* bringing selective sanctions to bear on random behaviour (as innumerable pedagogic psychologists have demonstrated), there is little evidence of such teaching playing an important role in the ordinary life of non-human species, particularly the less sophisticated ones. On the other hand, it seems obvious that this type of learning figures a good deal in the life of human beings. Can we say anything about the *significance* of this role?

6.1 *'Tradition'*.   The significance is, it may be argued, that, together with imitative learning, learning from teaching constitutes *a new mechanism of heredity*. Without learning of this kind, behaviour patterns can be passed from one generation to another only so long as they are specified, more or less precisely, in the genes; but *with* such learning transmission can occur across the generations without the genes being involved. The process of a group of animals adapting to changes in the environment is thus vastly speeded up — for instead of being dependent on natural selection, which requires generation upon generation, the establishment of a successful response throughout the group can be accomplished in the generation of its first discovery, and it can be passed down directly to the generations that follow. Learning from others is thus an evolutionary development of absolutely major importance.

The handing on of behaviour patterns — ways of doing things, or *customs* as we sometimes say — from one generation to the next is, one may say, the core of what is referred to by the term 'tradition' or 'culture'. A group has a *tradition* when its way of life has been handed down to it from previous generations. In a word, then, it is tradition that learning from others brings with it. And thus we arrive at the final suggestion about man's uniqueness that we are to consider: that it is precisely *tradition* that is the peculiarity of human life.

Such an idea is perhaps prejudiced by what we have said already, in arguing that the possibility of tradition arises whenever there is the possibility of one individual learning from others, and in allowing that this type of learning is not unique to man. And indeed, when one goes beyond possibilities to ask whether we know of any actual cases of behaviour patterns being transmitted by 'tradition' among non-human animals, the answer seems to be Yes.

Different troops of the Japanese monkey *Macaca fuscata*, just to take one example, have been shown to have quite different feeding habits, which have been observed to be transmitted 'culturally'. It is claimed, indeed, that the *origin* of a particular food habit and its subsequent establishment as part of one particular troop's tradition has been actually observed: a young female monkey was seen dipping her usual food — a sweet potato — in water before eating it, and her behaviour was then seen to be copied by other members of the troop until it became part of their way of life. Among other primates evidence for the occurrence of 'cultural' transmission seems just as clear, and as I have hinted some writers make out a case for its occurring much lower down in the evolutionary scale.

If we are looking for something absolutely peculiar to the human species, therefore, it does not seem that we have found it in the occurrence of 'tradition' or 'culture' — at least in the minimal sense of non-genetic transmission of behaviour patterns across the generations.

7 *Concluding remarks*

Perhaps, indeed, none of the attempts to identify man's uniqueness that we have considered is illuminating: that human beings are in physical terms uniquely independent of the environment; that they lack instincts; that they have recourse to 'insight' as well as to trial-and-error learning; that they possess a uniquely sophisticated language, enabling them to theorize; that their ability to learn by imitating others and by responding to others' teaching creates the possibility of tradition. All these ideas have certainly been challenged, and one can only go into the arguments and consider the evidence that I hardly have space even to outline here. But my own feeling is that Bennett — alongside many others, of course — is right in pointing to human language as having a quite special character, and that it was this evolutionary development among animals which were capable of *learning from teaching* that was crucial in creating human life as we know it. For these special linguistic powers, which I have tried to indicate above, would make of tradition something correspondingly special. The very sophisticated behaviour patterns we call 'general statements', for example, which, it is argued, are the basis of reasoning, could be elaborated and articulated in the light of successive generations' gradually accumulating experience — a tremendous potential that is tapped most obviously perhaps by the enterprise of science.

To the profound importance of human language and its bearing on the conduct of social study we shall shortly return, as we take now a new approach to the question of the distinctive nature of human life and explore the idea that what is special about the human being is the world of *meaning* that he alone inhabits.

5 Meaningful behaviour

1 *Introduction*

In his fine novel *Lord of the Flies* William Golding tells the story of a crowd of schoolboys, shipwrecked on a desert island. Beginning as a close-knit cooperating community, the group is subjected to tensions which eventually split it into warring factions. Golding 'symbolizes' the forces of disruption by introducing the idea of a Beast, which the boys come to think of as living on the island, ready and threatening to destroy them. The beginning of their dissension is marked by one of the younger children tearfully explaining how he saw a 'snake thing' in the night. And then, when Golding has shown the reality of the Beast growing in their imaginings, two of them see a moving shape on top of the mountain — and rush away hysterically, gasping to the others how they have actually *seen* 'the Beast'.

The being on the top of the mountain thus becomes the focus of the children's terror. Their actions are guided by their fear of annoying it, sacrifices are made to appease it, nightmares dominated by imagining what it intends to do with them.

Eventually one of their number, Simon, cast by Golding in the role of a Saviour, climbs the mountain, on his own, in order to attempt a confrontation with the source of their miseries: and confirms his suspicion that whatever beast there was, it did not live on top of a mountain. He discovers there instead the decaying body of a long-dead parachutist, still strapped to his parachute, rhythmically swaying to and fro by some trick of the wind.

What I want to remark on in this episode is the absolute difference in attitude that the boy's discovery brought about, at least for the only one who knew about it, Simon himself.

No longer a malevolent power to be appeased, the thing on the mountain top can simply be forgotten, left to the worms and the wind. Where before there had always to be the question of what the Beast wanted, of whether the Beast would be annoyed, of what the Beast would do, *now* these questions were simply inappropriate. The 'Beast' had turned out to be an unthinking thing, not a being capable of intending to do things, of having motives, of formulating plans. It had turned out to be nothing but a mass of decaying flesh caught in a tangle of lines.

To say exactly what is so terrifying about a Beast waiting up there on the mountain-top is, I think, not easy; what *is* clear, though, is that all fears (in this respect) are immediately dissipated once the Beast turns out to be a purely inanimate thing simply flapping in the breeze.

At the back of our relief, it may be tempting to think, is the realization that there is *nothing* at the back of the flapping. There is no *purpose* behind it, it is not performed with any *intention* in mind, there was no *motivation* informing it. The question of what whatever-it-is 'means to do', a desperate worry if the 'thing' is a Beast, simply does not arise.

These points can be reformulated, more helpfully from our point of view, in terms of explanation. If we think the movement on the mountain-top is the Beast, our demand to know why it is moving about, just like our demand for an explanation of any other part of its behaviour, will be looking for an answer in terms of the creature's purposes, its motives, intentions, plans — the considerations or reasons that weigh with it. But once we realize that the movement is nothing but the flapping of the harness, our asking why the flapping occurs will require an explanation in terms of the principles of mechanics — we shall want to know exactly how the arrangement of the straps and the blowing of the wind in a particular direction with a particular force resulted in the movement in question.

The importance of the contrast I have been dwelling on here — between one's attitude to a being, let us say, and one's attitude to an inanimate thing — is, perhaps obviously, that it is merely a dramatization of a certain contrast in the feelings we have in our everyday lives. All the time we recognize a difference, that is to say, between inanimate objects and *other people*, and behave very differently depending on which we think we are dealing with.

It is this contrast, recognized intuitively, I am suggesting, all the time, which I think writers have attempted to mark by the phrase 'meaningful behaviour'. There is thus said to be a distinction between behaviour that is 'meaningful' and behaviour that is 'non-meaningful'; and it is suggested by one influential school of thought, along the lines I have already sketched, that different kinds of explanation are called for in the two cases. As a consequence of this it is argued that the study of the two types of 'phenomena' can only be essentially different enterprises, and that any attempt to apply the methods appropriate to the one — which belongs to natural science — to the other — the study of human activity — must end in complete misunderstanding.

A good deal, then, hangs on the distinction I have been trying to illustrate, so that it is important as well as interesting to search beneath our intuitions for their foundations. What in exact terms is it that makes us judge human behaviour to be distinctive?

2 *Intentions*

Let us begin by considering in a precise form the suggestion that is clearly raised by the discussion so far: that meaningful behaviour should be identified with behaviour which has an *intention* behind it, and that whereas we attempt to explain meaningful behaviour in terms of *causes*, it is to *intentions* that we look in the case of behaviour that is 'meaningful'. In this way it is exactly the question of what the thing on the mountain-top *intends to do* that dissolves once its behaviour is revealed as not 'meaningful' at all.

We can accept this thesis, however, without going on to conclude that the study of meaningful behaviour must therefore be unique in character. For although it may be true that we should look for intentions in our attempts to explain it, there is no reason to think that explanations in terms of intentions differ fundamentally from those that are appropriate in the case of inanimate objects. Intentions, it might be said, are simply a species of *cause*, and explanations citing them simply a sort of causal explanation. It would then follow that the science of meaningful behaviour is not fundamentally different from the science of inanimate things.

Suppose, for example, my brother taps on my bedroom window in the middle of the night. When in due course I come to ask him why he did so I shall surely be asking what *caused* him to behave in this way; and the answer may be that he was *intending* to give me a scare in repayment of an old debt. Must we not therefore admit that in this case at least the *cause* of his tapping was his *intention* to frighten me?

It is argued by many, however, that our ordinary way of talking is misleading here. It may be true that we sometimes *speak* of intentions as causes; but when we think carefully we shall see important differences between intentions on the one hand and, let us say, the *type* of causes investigated by the natural scientist on the other.

Think of the man who celebrates his retirement by taking a Mediterranean cruise. 'I've been intending to do this all my life,' he may say. Is it plausible to think of his intention here as the *cause* of his taking the cruise? It would at least be an extraordinarily long-drawn-out one.

Or think of the conscientious Minister who receives the agenda for the weekly cabinet meeting. In normal circumstances no *decision* whether to attend it has to be made, since he attends such meetings as a matter of course, and yet although the question of attendance may never have crossed his mind it remains true that he intends to go. He intended to go from the moment he had notice of the meeting, but not because of any event or process which could be described as 'forming an intention'. Once again, to think of an intention as a cause, it has been argued, seems inappropriate.

Or call to mind the concert pianist, playing a difficult scherzo. Every note he plays he intends to play; yet the idea of each movement of his fingers being brought about by an intention formed by the mind in the split second between one note and the next is surely ludicrous.

A different argument is that an intention is not *distinct* from the action it informs in the way that a 'physical' cause is distinct from its effect. Perhaps the generation of a tidal wave by an earthquake gives us an unexceptional case of a 'physical' causal relationship; and we can see in such a case the sense in which its two participants are 'separate' events: the development of the wave is one happening, the convulsion of the underlying rock strata is another. The causal statement asserts that one of these two events brought about the other.

David Hume, whose writings in this connection have been extremely influential, implied that all genuine causal relationships exhibit this basic pattern; essentially involving *events* that are *distinct* from each other.

The first part of this claim is relatively clear — that the participants of causal relationships are events — but the second, that such events must be *distinct*, may need a word of explanation. Let me try to clarify the point, therefore, by giving an example of a pair of events which are *not* distinct in the relevant sense, and so, on Hume's view, not capable of being related causally. Think of my accidentally dropping a loaded breakfast tray. In dropping the loaded tray I drop, among the rest of the things, the teapot. But dropping the teapot is not an event distinct from dropping the loaded tray as a whole. (Dropping the teapot is, in a sense, 'part of' dropping the loaded tray.) For this reason alone (although there are others) Hume would think it senseless to wonder if dropping the teapot were the *cause* of dropping the tray as a whole. For the cause we have to look instead among distinct events: perhaps it was someone's jogging my elbow.

Or think of an accident in which the front of my car is smashed; and in which as a particular element of the general damage the left headlight is destroyed. According to Hume's principles once again, one cannot sensibly wonder whether the left headlight's being damaged was the cause of the entire car front's being damaged, since the two events mentioned are not distinct: one is 'part of' the other. It is argued that when we apply Hume's principle to the case of human behaviour we see that an intention and the action it informs are not events that are distinct from each other either.

We can think again of the pianist example in this light. The pianist plays each note *intentionally*, but are we to believe that the intention is an item separate from the playing? The thesis that action and intention are not distinct comes out most clearly, however (so some say), when the question is raised of how intentions are *identified*.

Very often, one cannot refer to an intention without referring to the action it informs; and this shows, it is said, that the intention and the action are not distinct items.

It would be true, for instance, of someone who was having a game of chess just for fun that he was doing what he was doing intentionally. But if we ask what his intention was we can only describe it or identify it by referring to the action of playing the game. What was his intention? To play a game of chess.

Whatever the conclusions we draw from arguments about intentions and intentional behaviour they make one thing clear: that the notion of behaviour behind which there is an intention is far from straightforward. In suggesting that what is distinctive about human behaviour is that it is intentional, therefore, we are initiating a line of thought rather than offering a complete answer. How might the thought be developed?

3 *Sense*

The patriarch of sociology, Max Weber, chose to couch his account in terms of 'meaning' and 'sense' rather than 'intention', but his ideas belong to this approach. In his view, what is distinctive about the actions of human beings is that the agent or 'actor' attaches to them a 'sense'.

Some have taken Weber to mean that what gives a particular piece of behaviour its distinctively human quality is the fact that behind it lies a certain process of *thought*. A weaver bird uses a twig to poke insects out of cracks in the bark of a tree, but the behaviour is not meaningful, because the bird does not (it is assumed) *think* about what it is doing but behaves by 'instinct'. The human being using a toothpick, on the other hand, may confront the problem of dental hygiene or discomfort mentally, and act in the light of such deliberation.

For this intuitively appealing approach the problem that arises, however, is that some actions seem to our intuitions to be perfectly meaningful, perfectly typical of human behaviour, and yet not to have had their meaning 'put into them', as it were, by the thinking of the agents who perform them. Peter Winch invites us to consider a person casting his vote — a person who has not given the least thought to *how* he should vote; someone who is simply unquestioningly following the example of his father and friends, and who, subsequently, no matter how hard he is pressed, can offer no reason for voting in the way he did. Even though such a person does not invest what he does with meaning or sense by any prior process of conscious thought, Winch asks, is it not true none the less that his voting *does* have a dimension of meaning? 'What he does is not *simply* to make a mark on a piece of paper,' says Winch, 'he is *casting a vote.*'

A further example borrowed by Winch from Freud argues the same point even more clearly:

> N forgets to post a letter and insists, even after reflection, that this was 'just an oversight' and had no reason. A Freudian observer might insist that N 'must have had a reason' even though it was not apparent to N: suggesting perhaps that N unconsciously connected the posting of the letter with something in his life which is painful and which he wants to suppress.

Here again, if we allow the possibility of the Freudian account, we seem prepared to treat an action — something a human being has done (or, better in this case, omitted to do) — as meaningful, in spite of the absence of related conscious processes of thought.

Actions can be meaningful, Winch concludes (and he argues that a proper understanding of Weber shows that he too appreciated the point), even though no sense is attached to them by the conscious thought of the agent concerned. The problem of explaining in what their 'meaningfulness' consists therefore remains.

4 *Action*

The solution that Winch himself develops begins by noticing that the distinction we are trying to fathom seems to be partially reflected in a difference in our way of referring to the two allegedly different sorts of behaviour. Behaviour that is distinctive of human beings is always a matter of human *action*; whereas happenings in the inanimate world are spoken of as *events*. A twig striking my window pane and a parachute harness taughtening in the wind are both *events*, and they contrast with the *actions* of my brother tapping on the window, and the Beast threatening the shipwrecked schoolboys.

We must not jump to the conclusion, though, that the categories of events and actions sit side by side as though whatever happens is exclusively either one or the other. For it seems natural to say that the action of tapping on the window *involves* an event — a certain movement of the arm — so that instead of speaking of happenings as being divisible exclusively into actions and events we should regard actions as simply a special kind of event.

It seems typical of actions, in fact, that they involve bodily movements. When I wave a greeting, my arm moves; when I get up and close the door, my body moves; I cannot kick a football without moving my leg. But, more interesting than this, there are cases where one and the same bodily movement performed in different contexts can represent different actions.

The bad driver whose hand signals are vague and who is also given to greeting friends on the pavement with a wave of the arm provides a practical example. It may be that the bodily movement he engages in when waving to a friend is exactly the same as the movement he makes as a signal of his intention to turn left. Another road user cannot tell which action it is: therein, of course, lies its danger.

Think, for a slightly different example, of the bodily movements involved in writing your signature; and then think of the great variety of different actions those bodily movements can represent: giving away your fortune (when they constitute signing a comprehensive cheque), resigning from your job (when they constitute signing a letter of resignation), declaring war (if you are Foreign Secretary putting your name to the appropriate document), an attempt to teach a child to write, trying out a new pen, etc.

What is it, then, that makes the same bodily movement (or set of bodily movements) one action on one occasion, and another action on another?

5 *Actions and rules*

Turning the question the other way round, we may ask: what is it that makes, for example, a particular movement of the hand in some circumstances a hand signal?

A plausible answer is that it is a *convention*. People using the roads, or their representatives, have come to an agreement, formulated explicitly in the Highway Code, that a certain kind of bodily movement shall constitute a signal of the kind in question. No 'convention' making a certain movement of the arm a friendly wave is explicitly formulated (it may then be conceded) but the wave nevertheless derives its meaning in a similar way. People in a society have come to a *tacit* agreement that under certain circumstances a certain kind of arm movement shall constitute a greeting. We can easily imagine a different agreement being reached. Think of the belch, a piece of rudeness in the West, a gesture of warm appreciation in some other cultures.

In cases such as these, one might say that there is (in a particular culture) a rule relating a particular piece of bodily behaviour to a set of circumstances: a rule by virtue of which that behaviour, done in those circumstances, is meaningful. There is, to revert to our example, a rule that a certain movement of the arm, on the part of a man driving a car and intending to turn left, shall constitute a signal of the driver's intention. Likewise, there is a tacit rule in some cultures that an expulsion of wind following a meal is a mark of appreciation.

Some writers, of which Winch is one, take cases of this kind as hints towards an understanding of human action in general. What converts a 'mere' bodily movement into a meaningful action, it is claimed, is the performance of the bodily movement in accordance with some *rule*: meaningful action is *rule-governed behaviour*.

Take the example of your fingers moving so as to make a pen write your name. For this to be a case of signing a cheque, say, certain conditions have to be met. The paper you are marking must (these days) be a sheet issued by a bank for the purpose; it must not (in the usual case) have someone else's signature already on it; you must put your name in the bottom right-hand corner. Also, your efforts won't be completely successful if you make a slip in the signature and fail to initial the correction; or if you don't use the form of signature that you used when you gave a specimen signature to open your account — for in such cases, it will be said, you have not signed the cheque 'properly'. These, then, it might be claimed, are some of the rules which, when adhered to, make certain movements of the pen in your fingers *signing a cheque*.

Winch offers two further arguments in support of the contention that what is distinctive of meaningful actions is their rule-guidedness. First, he says, the simple observation that we can speak of meaningful actions being performed *correctly* or *incorrectly* is enough to show that we are 'applying criteria' or following a rule. His example (which he derives from Wittgenstein) is *counting*. In learning to count it is not enough to be able to repeat the counting of our teacher; we must know how to carry on counting at the point where he leaves off. If he rehearses '1,2,3,4,5' we must be able not only to repeat '1,2,3,4,5' but to carry on independently '6,7,8,9,10', and so on. There are an indefinite number of ways in which we might carry on wrongly: '6,7,10,9,8' would be one of them. What we have to grasp, therefore, is a test or criterion that enables us to know which number comes next; so that making a mistake in our counting will be misapplying this criterion. It is true of meaningful human actions in general, claims Winch, that we can speak of doing them correctly or incorrectly; and it follows from this that all meaningful human action must be rule-governed.

A second argument to be found in *The Idea of a Social Science* is that in acting meaningfully we necessarily commit ourselves to acting in a particular way in the future, and that this can only be so if our acting is the application of a rule. Think of my handing over to the bus-conductor a small circular piece of nickel silver with the Queen's head stamped on it. This transaction becomes an action of payment only if I am tacitly undertaking to accept such a piece of metal in return for services I myself might render in the future. Pieces of metal, it might be said, only become coins by virtue of a general agreement to use them in a certain way. Or think of my placing a slip of paper between the leaves of a book, which becomes a case of *using a bookmark* only if I do so with the idea of using the slip to determine where I am to start reading again at some future time. Winch thinks these cases are typical of actions in respect of committing the actor to behaving in a particular way in the future. Performing a particular action, in other words, involves applying a rule which links present to future behaviour; so that once more we have the conclusion that action is necessarily *rule-guided*.

6 *Rules, words and understanding*

The suggestion that what is distinctive in human action is to be understood in terms of rules is illuminated by the further thought that it is *rules* that give words their meaning too.

Think for example of the sound made when someone utters the

word 'tree'. To learn this word, a child would have to learn when it is appropriate to make such a sound and when it is not. If he utters the sound arbitrarily, without rhyme or reason, he cannot be said to have learnt the word at all; and saying 'that is a tree' when pointing to a lamp-post or a forget-me-not would be inappropriate and a teacher would have to make this clear. One might say that what the child has to learn is a rule that relates the noise associated with the word 'tree' to a certain set of circumstances. To learn the word's meaning is to learn the rule.

If valid, therefore, Winch's arguments about actions show that they are like words, in that both are governed by rules. Human activity, it is thus argued, is like talking — it is 'quasi-linguistic'. Thus we are provided with a rationale for the description of distinctively human behaviour as 'meaningful'. The rules governing it endow it with meaning just as words derive their meaning from the rules that govern them.

The important consequence is, of course, that, because they are rule-guided, actions call for a type of understanding that has more in common with understanding language than with understanding the interactions of inanimate objects as pursued by natural science. Somebody bringing to social study the attitudes of natural science would try simply to offer a *causal* explanation for a piece of human behaviour, but, it is claimed, behaviour that is rule-guided cannot adequately be understood in that way.

One aspect of the significance of the difference between being governed by rules and being subject to causal laws emerges from the fact that rules can be broken but laws cannot. If an object is identified as behaving inconsistently with what has been thought to be a causal law, the latter is discredited; but a person driving while drunk has no tendency to show that the rule — in this case a law of the land — against drunken driving is invalid.

Rules can thus be 'misapplied' as well as applied — and this indicates what is perhaps, in the present context, the central point about them: they involve *agents*. A rule cannot be followed unless there is someone to follow it; so that, against the conception of the human being as a complex object belonging to a network of objects and processes locked causally together, the view that actions are rule-guided maintains the conception of autonomous human agents guiding their behaviour in the light of rules.

There is allegedly a further connection between actions and language, however, that we have yet to make clear. Not only, it is said, are actions, like words, governed by rules, but where we have a word *for* an action (and we always have) the rules governing it will include the rules that govern that action itself.

For example, one of the rules that makes a certain movement of the arm a case of giving a traffic signal of a particular sort is that one must be the driver of some vehicle. But it follows that we shall be wrong to use the term 'traffic signal' in connection with activity performed by someone who is *not* driving a vehicle.

The rules that make a piece of behaviour a certain action are reflected, therefore (so it is argued), in the rules governing the 'concept' of the action. When it is claimed, therefore, that social study has a 'conceptual dimension', or when it is claimed that the understanding of an action involves understanding *meanings*, there are two reinforcing points being made: first that actions are rule-guided and thus call for a quasi-linguistic understanding, and second that the rules that guide them are embodied in the rules that govern their associated concepts, and can thus be identified by studying those concepts.

When we observe the social world, then, it may be that what we observe is partially created — given its structure, one might say — by human conceptual thought.

But concepts are sometimes said to enter into our experience of the world, including other people, also in a rather different way, and this we turn to next.

6 The framework of experience

1 *Introduction: a visual analogy*

If the world as its inhabitants actually perceive it is partially the creation of their own language, their behaviour will be influenced by their language too, and any attempt to understand or explain that behaviour must take this 'conceptual dimension' into account. We now explore an idea about the relation between our concepts and how we see the world around us which therefore has basic implications for any study of human beings.

It is easy to think of the human being as surrounded by the familiar world of buildings, dogs, furniture, and so on, which he only has to open his eyes to see, or extend his hands to touch. His mind can thus be regarded as a kind of collecting box with the slot in the top representing the senses, through which the small change of experience passively drops — images falling on the retina, sounds on the eardrum, taste-sensations on the taste-buds. In earlier days they put it in terms of a different simile. They said the mind was like a *tabula rasa*, a plain writing block, on which stimuli, penetrating through the senses, wrote their different messages. But the principle is the same: the organs of sense are regarded as passive receivers of impressions impinging from without.

Though those of us who are not psychologists may slip into this way of thinking, a number of things should give us pause. One is the disturbing experience of the person who was born blind and by some surgical technique is given his sight half-way through life. Now according to the view which regards the senses as passive receivers we should expect a person cured in this way to have no trouble at all. He would simply open his eyes and receive impressions from the world around him just like the rest of us. But in fact such a person spends many hours after opening his eyes in great distress and confusion, before his visual experience in the end becomes ordered and undisturbing. Seeing, it is suggested by cases of this kind, so far from being a passive business, is more like a sophisticated activity that has to be *learnt*.

Anybody who has had to study things with the aid of a microscope will have had first-hand experience of these complexities. Your instructor tells you to look in a particular area for the feature in question; he looks himself to check; but you, the learner, just can't see it. 'It's there,' he insists, 'just above the blue spot': you look, and look again, but see nothing. And then, perhaps, you *do* see it, and can only wonder however you could possibly have missed it. The answer is, you had to *learn* to see it.

This is why, it seems plausible to think, paintings we are not used to, particularly if they are cast in a new style, very often mean almost nothing to us at first sight. How ridiculous that we should be required to pronounce a verdict on a new picture after a few seconds' appraisal! Yet this we are often urged to do, even by the artist himself. 'For goodness sake say *something*!' we are entreated. 'Either you like it or you don't.' But perhaps the fact of the matter is that we don't know whether we like it or not the first time we 'see' it; for the first time we hardly 'see' it at all. It's only by looking at it again — and again and again — that we gradually come to *see* what's in the picture, and therefore begin to be in a position to say whether we like what we see there or not. 'Seeing what's there', it is thus suggested, is a considerable achievement, and it's only the few who are practised and perhaps the very few who don't need to be who can pull it off within the space of a few seconds.

In my next example I want to be more specific and mention a particular respect in which the eye is active in perception. I want to put forward the suggestion that it holds up to the outside world a kind of stencil, which allows some elements in and keeps others out, according to a pre-existent pattern. Take the case of my seeing a rhinoceros, for example. Put crudely, the business of seeing a rhinoceros is composed of two parts. One contribution is made by the external world — including the rhinoceros. Its 'image', among a multitude of other impressions, impinges upon me; but *I* also make a contribution. I have an idea of what the rhinoceros is like, and my actual visual experience is a result of the interaction between the image that impinges, as it were, and my idea. You could say my idea acts as a sort of templet, held up between me and the world, which picks out from the chaotic blur of impressions before me just the ones I proceed to call those of a rhinoceros.

This understanding of perception is given much attention by the art historian E. H. Gombrich in his brilliant and fascinating book *Art and Illusion*. He calls the 'templets' or 'ideas' to which I have just referred schemata, and his point is that learning to see involves building up schemata, the templets through which we see the world, and which together structure our visual experience.

By way of illustration he tells us about two attempts, one two and a half centuries after the other, to *draw* the rhinoceros. The first was by Albrecht Dürer. 'When Dürer published his famous woodcut of a rhinoceros,' Gombrich tells us, 'he had to rely on secondhand evidence which he filled in from his own imagination, coloured, no doubt, by what he had learned of the most famous of exotic beasts, the dragon with its armoured body. Yet it has been shown', he goes on, 'that this half-invented creature served as a model for all renderings of the rhinoceros, even in natural history books, up to the eighteenth century.' Gombrich is saying here that Dürer's woodcut did much to establish man's 'schema' of the rhinoceros, so that whenever he saw one he saw it 'through Dürer's eyes'. He saw it 'through' the idea or templet that Dürer's woodcut provided.

In 1790 James Bruce published alongside his own engraving of the rhinoceros an appreciation of the fact that Dürer's picture had been the source of a good deal of error in later drawings. Bruce writes:

The animal represented in this drawing [Bruce's own] ... is the first drawing of the rhinoceros with a double horn that has ever yet been presented to the public. The first figure of the Asiatic rhinoceros, the species having but one horn, was painted by Albert Dürer, from the life. ... It was wonderfully ill-executed in all its parts, and was the origin of all the monstrous forms under which that animal has been painted, ever since. ... Several modern philosophers have made amends for this in our days; Mr Parsons, Mr Edwards, and the Count de Buffon have given good figures of it from life; they have indeed some faults, owing chiefly to preconceived prejudices and inattention. ... This ... is the first that has been published with two horns, it is designed from life, and is an African.

So ends Bruce's remarks. Gombrich prints side by side the Dürer, the Bruce picture (so proudly presented in the words just quoted) and a modern photograph (Figure 2). Now what one would expect is that the Bruce picture and the photograph would be similar, while

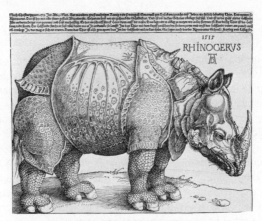

Dürer, *Rhinoceros* (1515). Woodcut.

Heath, *Rhinoceros of Africa* (1789).
Engraving from James Bruce, *Travels to Discover the Source of the Nile* (1790).

African rhinoceros. Photograph.

Fig 2 Perception structured by schemata
(From E. H. Gombrich, *Art and Illusion*, p. 71)

the Dürer would be the odd one out. But this is not at all the case. It is the *photograph* which is odd and the two pictures, the Dürer and the Bruce, which are similar. In spite of all his words, Bruce has clearly derived the scheme for his engraving from the Dürer. The Dürer created a schema through which people saw the rhinoceros whether they realized it or not; indeed, it determined the way they saw a rhinoceros even when they consciously tried to reject it.

What Gombrich is arguing is that in our visual perception we meet the world half-way. Goethe put it by saying 'experience is but half of experience'. The world comes at us as a chaotic welter of impressions which we fend off with a kind of sieve, or framework, or set of categories, or schemata, which impose a certain order on those impressions, and give them a kind of structure; as an end product there is generated the world as we experience it. 'Without some starting point,' he writes, 'some initial schema, we could never get hold of the flux of experience. Without categories, we could not sort our impressions.'

2 *Experience structured by concepts*

This conception of perception, if at all valid, at least complicates our notion of simple observation and what findings we can base on it. But it also gives us a way of understanding a more general thesis about the relationship between man and his experience of the world. For just as schemata structure our visual perception, it is claimed, so *language* structures our experience in general.

In other words, we grasp the world through our conceptual apparatus, without which experience would not be experience; it would be completely undiscriminated, unintelligible. Our system of concepts imposes categories, divides experience into discrete items between which relationships become possible. So far from merely labelling prediscriminated entities, our concepts make their discrimination possible. Gombrich himself makes the point without developing it (since it is off his main theme): 'Language does not give names to pre-existing things or concepts so much as it articulates the world of our experience.'

So, according to this view, language acts as a framework on which reality as we know it is hung; or, like a cheese-grater, dividing an amorphous mass into discrete parts; or, better, it is like a grid through which reality is perceived.

This view implies, of course, that two people with different conceptual frameworks will 'experience reality' in different ways, and also that some feature of our experience may reflect not as we may think the world about us but the nature of our own conceptual apparatus. Later we shall return to this second line of thought.

But what of the first? Do people with importantly different languages and therefore different conceptual schemes experience the world in different ways?

2.1 *Anthropological understanding*. Rodney Needham in his introduction to Durkheim and Mauss's book *Primitive Classification* argues that this is very much the case. He begins by describing, as we did, the desperate situation of the congenitally blind person who becomes sighted half-way through life. Such a man, says Needham, immediately after the operation, 'is afflicted by a painful chaos of forms and colours, a gaudy confusion of visual impressions none of which seems to bear any comprehensible relationship to the others. Only very slowly and with intense effort can he teach himself that this confusion does indeed manifest an order, and only by resolute application does he learn to distinguish and classify objects and acquire the meaning of terms such as "space" and "shape".' Then Needham comes to his point:

> When an ethnographer begins his study of a strange people he is in a remarkably analogous position, and in the case of an unknown society he may exactly, in no trite sense, be described as culturally blind. He is confronted with a confusion of foreign impressions none of which can safely be assumed to be what they appear, and the contrast between these and the usages of his own society may be so jarring as even to induce a sense of shock. It is only with the most arduous and protracted efforts that he can grasp something of how the people he is trying to understand 'see' themselves and the world in which they live, and not until he has achieved this can he usefully proceed to the technical investigations proper to his academic subject.

For, Needham explains, the ethnographer carries with him into the strange culture

> ... such concepts as 'god', 'power', 'debt', 'family', 'gift', and so on, and however thorough his professional preparation he will tend at first to look for and identify what his own culture denotes by these words and to interpret the statements in terms of them. But gradually he learns to see the world as it is constituted for the people themselves, to assimilate their distinctive categories. Typically, he may have to abandon the distinction between the natural and the supernatural, relocate the line between life and

death, accept a common nature in mankind and animals. He cannot pretend to perceive the phenomena involved in any entirely new way, but he can and must conceptualize them in this foreign cast. ... Learning the language teaches him to do this.

The language of a people, then, helps determine their mode of experience — that is Needham's notion, and it is one that several thinkers have taken seriously. Perhaps we can give more body to it by considering an example from the work of its great pioneer, Benjamin Lee Whorf.

2.2 *The experience of time.* Whorf developed his theories for the most part in terms of a comparison between ourselves, people of the industrial West, and the American Indian Hopi people, whose language and conceptual structure he claimed to be radically different from ours.

One way in which we differ is in our attitude to time. Our tense system helps to make us 'objectify' or 'spatialize' time. When we speak of past, present and future it's easy for us to think of time as a kind of clothes-line, with the pole — the present — in the middle and successive days, for example, strung out along its length like so many pegs. We *count* days, just as we count pegs, using the cardinal numbers. That is, we imagine days sitting side by side in an aggregate, and we count 'one, two, three ... ' Seven days, to shift the simile, are like seven men: seven separate items which we can think of as standing side by side.

But the Hopi way of thinking is quite different. They do not think of time in *spatial* terms, as we do. They use no spatial metaphors. They have no tenses to their verbs, and they express what we express by tense differences in other ways. Moreover, where we should count days using cardinals, they use the ordinals — 'first, second, third ... '

In consequence, the Hopi and the Westerner behave very differently to the 'passage of time'. The difference is best explained in terms of the analogy we have already mentioned. If we liken a day to the visit of a man then the difference is this: while we behave to the passage of ten days as though each day were the visit of a different man, the Hopi think of ten days as though it were the same man visiting on ten different occasions.

The practical consequences of this different conceptual framework are, claims Whorf, profound. If one thinks of time as we do in the West, on the analogy of several different men visiting one after the other, then whatever we do today will not have much influence on what happens next week. That is, you don't alter the sort of man that turns up next by interfering with his predecessor. But if it's the *same* man who is going to turn up again and again and again, then there is every sense in which one can affect how he is on his next visit by interfering with him now. And so it is, Whorf explains, that the Hopi way of life is much preoccupied with ritual and preparatory exercises, since they are led to deal with the future by working within the present situation, which is supposed to carry impresses forward into the future and so affect the event which is of particular interest.

2.3 *Theories in science.*   A further interesting case of a 'relativist' view of the kind we have been discussing is provided by T. S. Kuhn, though his argument is developed not so much in relation to different cultures or different religions but in respect of different theories within science.

A scientist in normal circumstances is held by Kuhn to work within a 'paradigm' — a theoretical framework which he shares with the other workers in the field at that particular time. Such a framework represents the categories through which the scientists' experience is gained, and scientists with different paradigms will have, according to Kuhn, different experiences by virtue of that fact.

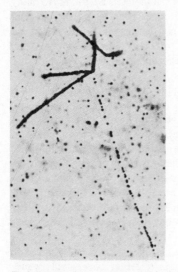

Fig 3 From a photomicrograph of tracks
made by nuclear particles in
emulsion (J. H. Fremlin,
Applications of Nuclear Physics,
Plate IX, facing p. 149)

Two examples may help to make clear what Kuhn means. First, consider the sketch shown in Figure 3 taken from a photograph belonging to a research paper in nuclear physics. The paper, we should note, purports to be a straightforward experimental report: it sets out simply to record 'the facts'. Below the photograph, as a description of it, we read: '"Thorium star" in G5 emulsion. α-tracks from the decay of the thorium decay-product Th^{228} and its descendants. ... The slight separation due to diffusion ... can be seen. The β-track from Bi^{212} can also be seen.'

All this caption is meant to do is describe, as a straightforward matter of observed fact, what has been photographed. Yet in this statement of a 'straightforward matter of observed fact' there occur concepts that did not exist a hundred years ago. 'Particle', 'α-particle', 'decay', etc., are the products of accepted theory, and in accepting the theory the scientist has committed himself to seeing things that those who reject the theory will not see.

The psychoanalyst Karen Horney in her book *Self-Analysis* provides us with a very different example of the same phenomenon. In the following passages she is giving us an account of the 'facts' of a patient's condition:

> The compulsive need to lean on a 'partner' appeared. ... Its main feature was an entirely repressed parasitic attitude, an unconscious wish to feed on the partner, to expect him to supply the content of her life, to take responsibility for her, to solve all her difficulties and to make her a great person without her having to make efforts of her own. This trend had alienated her not only from other people but also from the partner himself, because the unavoidable disappointment she felt when her secret expectations of him remained unfulfilled gave rise to deep inner irritation; most of this irritation was repressed for fear of losing the partner, but some of it emerged in occasional explosions.

The appropriateness of the expression 'theory-laden' in relation to the key terms being used here will be obvious. Concepts like 'repression', 'alienation', 'compulsive need', 'unconscious wish' are all heavily laden with psychoanalytic theory. Because this is the theoretical framework with which Horney approaches her patient, she sees her 'in these terms'. What she recognizes as, or acknowledges to be, observed facts are 'structured' by the conceptual apparatus with which she approaches her experience of the world.

2.4 *The relativity of truth.* In insisting that a scientist's conceptual framework enters into the formation of whatever is recognized by the scientist as a *fact*, Kuhn is turning the conventional understanding of science and scientific progress on its head. The facts that science tries to discover and then to explain, we might easily think, are objectively there in nature, and we can judge whether our theories are satisfactory by seeing whether they *fit* these facts. Kuhn is taking the 'relativist' position of saying that what we regard as the facts will differ according to the theories we hold.

But then, if scientists with different theoretical frameworks 'experience reality' in different ways, is it sensible to wonder which of these ways is correct? Indeed, if their experience of the world is always and necessarily mediated by a theoretical framework, does it make any sense to wonder what 'reality' is like, as it were, when it is *not* being grasped through a theoretical framework? To speak more positively, Kuhn's thesis that there are no theory-independent, 'neutral' facts against which to measure the correctness of any given framework carries the stupendous implication that all talk of theoretical frameworks being correct or incorrect, all talk of their being *true* or *untrue*, is really without sense. 'Truth' is then itself relative to paradigms. *Within* a given theoretical framework one can ask whether *this* is true, or whether *that* is a fact; but one can never compare two theoretical frameworks and ask whether one is more correct or in better accordance with the facts than the other. This means, for example, that the physicists of today cannot be said to know more than their ancestors did in medieval times, and, more generally, it means that science cannot be thought of as establishing, down the centuries, more and more of the truth about the universe.

Kuhn's thesis about the relativity of truth is developed specifically in connection with scientific theories, but an analogous conclusion is implied by any radical claim that our view of the world is created by our concepts. For on any such view it is impossible to get outside all conceptual schemes, impossible to describe reality as she 'really is', and thus impossible to achieve a position from which the truth of any claim made within a conceptual framework may be 'externally' assessed.

2.5 *The relativity of rationality.*   To those who hold that our conceptual framework creates, in the sense we have been exploring, our world — to 'relativists', let us say, for short — there are no 'objective' standards of truth. Nor, to move to a second point, can there be any 'objective' standards of rationality.

Within a conceptual scheme, it is acknowledged, we can defend our belief in this or that by appealing to considerations that others will acknowledge to be reasons (though perhaps not compelling) for holding the belief. I may, for example, defend my belief in evolution by appealing to the fossil record. Some might disagree with my conclusion, but they would agree with me that the fossil record is *relevant* to the idea of evolution, and they would be able to understand why a consideration of it should weigh with us. We agree over what counts as a reason for believing something. People with different conceptual frameworks need not agree even in this respect, however — the relativist argues.

The case may be put in terms of an example from the classic — and beautifully readable — study by the anthropologist E. E. Evans-Pritchard, *Witchcraft, Oracles and Magic among the Azande.* Among the Azande, a traditional people of Central Africa, the deliverances of the 'poison oracle' are often regarded as relevant to ascriptions of responsibility. If, for example, a man suspects his neighbour of bringing about the collapse of his house, he may arrange to consult the oracle, to confirm or disprove his suspicion. A fowl is taken and a quantity of the special substance *benge* administered to it. Then, addressing the *benge* within the fowl, the officiant instructs it, say, to kill the fowl should the suspicion be well founded, and let it live if not. The fate of the bird is then observed, and as a check the questions are reversed as more *benge* is administered to a second fowl. If the results are consistent — that is, if a fowl dies on one occasion but survives on the other — the 'judgement' the oracle has thus delivered will be appealed to as a reason for believing that the man was, or was not, responsible as alleged. To the contemporary Westerner, however — and this is the point of the example in this context — the fate of the fowls will seem simply irrelevant to the question at issue.

An illustration from a little nearer home is the rebuttal, by the astronomer Francesco Sizi, of Galileo's claim to have discovered that Jupiter was attended by satellites. The claim, argued Sizi, would imply the number of planets was greater than seven, which is enough to show that it must be wrong:

> There are seven windows in the head, two nostrils, two ears, two eyes and a mouth; so in the heavens there are two favourable stars, two unpropitious, two luminaries, and Mercury alone undecided and indifferent. From which and many other similar phenomena of nature, such as the seven metals, etc., which it were tedious to enumerate, we gather that the number of planets is necessarily seven.

Sizi goes on to offer a further consideration:

Moreover, the satellites are invisible to the naked eye and therefore can have no influence on the earth and therefore would be useless and therefore do not exist.

Sizi clearly means these remarks of his to be taken as *arguments*; but can he be right to do so? C. G. Hempel, from whose discussion I borrow the Sizi passages, declares that the 'defect' of Sizi's considerations is not difficult to see: 'The "facts" it adduces, even if accepted without question, are entirely irrelevant to the point at issue; they do not afford the slightest reason for the assumption that Jupiter has no satellites; the claim of relevance suggested by the barrage of words like "therefore", "it follows", and "necessarily" is entirely spurious.'

Hempel probably formulates our own reactions to Sizi's words. But what we have to remember is that Sizi was a serious man, not a mad one, adducing considerations which he hoped would convince his contemporaries that Galileo could not be right. And, of course, there were plenty of people at the time who thought the arguments Sizi put forward, and others of the same general kind, convincing enough. To them, Hempel's easy remark that 'the crucial defect [in what Sizi has to say] ... is evident' would be nonsense; and his round assertion that 'The "facts" it adduces ... are entirely irrelevant to the point at issue' would be condemned as itself evidently false.

The relativist will describe the situation by saying that Hempel and Sizi do not agree over what counts as a reason for holding a belief: they have different 'criteria of rationality'.

2.6 *The relativity of logic.*

There is a third fundamental respect in which conceptual structures may differ, on a relativist view, and that is as regards their *logic*. It is difficult to say quickly and clearly and uncontroversially what is a principle of logic, but an example of one would be that *no proposition can be both true and false* — the so-called 'law of non-contradiction'. The 'law of the excluded middle', that *if a proposition is not true then it must be false*, would be another. One might say that they are the principles in virtue of which valid arguments are valid.

Naïvely, one might think that whatever is a valid argument *here* must be a valid argument *anywhere* — that logical principles if true at all must be true universally. But this is just what the unreserved relativist questions. Our logical principles, it is suggested, may not hold elsewhere. What counts as valid in our culture may not count as valid in other cultures.

The anthropologist Lévy-Bruhl, for example, speaks of the logic

of those he calls 'primitives' as 'strange and even hostile' to that of
the world to which he himself belonged, and he points by way of
illustration to the saying of the Nuer that 'twins are birds'.

What can the Nuer mean when they point to human twins and call
them 'birds'? It is tempting for us to assume that they must be meaning to assert some *similarity* between human twins and birds, so that
they are really to be understood as saying 'twins are *like* birds in
certain respects'. But those who have studied the matter declare that
the words the Nuer use and the context in which they use them will
not allow this interpretation. They must be understood as saying not
that twins are *like* birds but that they *are* birds.

With this clear the Westerner might then wonder whether the Nuer
actually see any difference between twins and birds. Do they,
incredibly, have some psychological peculiarity which results in their
simply not being able to tell the difference between twins born of
human beings and birds? Again, the authority explains that this isn't
so. 'They are not saying', as Evans-Pritchard puts it, 'that a twin has
a beak, feathers, and so forth.'

But then, if they are prepared to acknowledge that twins are
different from birds — that they are *not* birds — how can they assert
that they *are*?

The solution that the throughgoing relativist puts forward is that
there is only a problem in making both these assertions on *our*
principles of logic, according to which they would see a contradiction between the two assertions 'a human twin is a bird' and 'a
human twin is not a bird' and feel forced to withdraw one (or both)
of the claims. That they don't feel this, but go on defending both,
shows (Lévy-Bruhl wants us to conclude) that they don't share our
logic.

2.7 *Some difficulties.*   There is more than one huge difficulty with
the unreservedly relativist view we have been considering. Can one
really accept the idea that truth is not something our scientific
theories strive after, but rather something each *defines*, and each in
its own way? Can one really accept the idea that there is no reality
independent of each culture's constructed realities? And if rationality — and, even more fundamentally, logic — were culture-bound,
how would cross-cultural communication or understanding ever take
place? Unless one made the assumption that speakers of a given
language recognized basic logical laws like the law of non-
contradiction it would surely be impossible to begin to translate it.
Finally, are we really prepared to accept that there could be no
independent *reasons* for preferring one conceptual framework to

another (say, the scientific to that of the Nuer)? For if what counts as a reason were determined within a culture this conclusion would indeed seem to follow.

These difficulties, insuperable to many, spring from the uncompromising character of the relativism we have been considering. Different cultures, different stages in the development of a science, have different conceptual frameworks; and there is no possibility of asking which of them 'does better justice to the facts' because there are no facts that are independent of any frameworks to be appealed to. But need relativism be so uncompromising? Might there be a way of retaining the valuable points that the thoroughgoing relativist seems to make in the course of his account while at the same time avoiding its more demanding implications?

7 The interpretation of experience

1 *Introduction*

There is something compelling in the examples the relativist offers, and something challenging about the arguments, even though the overall conclusion is unacceptable — this is the spirit of the idea we now consider. It suggests a line should be drawn between *facts* on the one hand and *interpretation* of the facts on the other. Our conceptual framework, on this weaker view, does not as it were *create* the facts, though it does deeply influence what one shall *make* of them. The suggestion, then, would be that two people with different conceptual frameworks may confront *the same* fact — which is impossible on the uncompromising view — but would be likely to interpret it differently. On such a view as this the more radical of the relativist's claims are not involved — yet some of the difficulty in saying which of two such frameworks 'does more justice' to the facts remains, as we shall see when we develop as an example a particularly fascinating case.

2 *The belief system of the Azande*

In the study of the Azande to which we have already referred, Evans-Pritchard explains the Azande concept of causation. The Azande believe that, in order to ensure the success of a venture, bringing to bear technical knowledge and skills is not enough. One possibility is that one's efforts may be thwarted by witchcraft, and one should take steps to guard against this eventuality by achieving friendly relations with one's neighbours, for example, and perhaps by having defensive rites conducted prior to undertaking the project. In order to ensure a good harvest, to take a particular case, it is considered necessary but not sufficient to see that the soil is well prepared, the seed well chosen and the moment of sowing and of reaping well judged. It is also necessary to conduct the traditional ritual.

From the standpoint of the scientifically minded Westerner, we might think it easy to show any fair-minded Azande that he must be mistaken in his belief about the efficacy of ritual. We need only invite him to confront the fact that even with consistently skilful husbandry there must be many years in which the harvest is disappointing *in spite of* the fact that the ritual had been performed. Surely this happens, the Westerner may say, and surely it demonstrates the invalidity of the Azande belief.

But the Azande conceptual scheme provides what the Westerner might describe as an escape route. Their belief is that in order for a good harvest to be secured the appropriate ritual must be performed *properly*, and one of the ways in which an attempt to perform the ritual *properly* may be thwarted is for someone to entertain 'evil thoughts'.

How do they tell when the ritual has been marred in this way? The Azande look for the proof of the pudding in the eating. If the harvest is a bad one in spite of the fact that every attempt had been made to conduct the correct ritual, they have a strong indication that someone's evil thoughts were frustrating their efforts.

The Azande's belief that properly performing the correct ritual helps ensure a good crop therefore survives confrontation with 'the facts'. It is protected by two further beliefs: that evil thoughts interfere with the proper performance of the rite, and that, when the crops fail after the rite has been performed, the occurrence of such evil thoughts at the ceremony is shown. As MacIntyre puts it, this interlocking set of beliefs means that 'there is never a year when it is unavoidable for them [the Azande] to admit that the rites were duly performed, but that they did not thrive.'

This is just a tiny part of the general case mounted by Evans-Pritchard for the conclusion that in the case of the Azande we can identify a network of beliefs which complement each other in such a way as to protect the world-view as a whole from 'facts', or better ways of looking at facts, which would disturb it. A failed harvest following the proper performance of the relevant rites would undermine belief in the rites' efficacy, and so the entire Azande world-view; but their conception of what constitutes the proper conduct of the rites and their notion of 'pollution' prevent them from ever having to see a failed harvest in this light. They accept the *fact* that harvests sometimes fail, but they interpret it in a way that preserves their system of beliefs.

We may perhaps be tempted to indulge in a sense of superiority when we view the elaborate defences that the Azande world-view throws up against experience. But before doing so it will perhaps be salutary to consider whether our own outlook is free of such devices.

3　*The principle of causality*

Think, for example, of the concept of causality. It is a basic belief of ours, it has often been said, that whatever happens is *caused* to happen. We acknowledge, that is to say, as a basic element of our conceptual scheme, what is usually called the *principle of causality*, the principle that *every event has a cause*. The question that I suggest we ask is: could our experience ever show that this principle was mistaken? Could we ever be persuaded by our observations of what happened in the world to give it up? Those who think we could should be able to say what we should have to observe to make us discard it; so we may ask: what would evidence against the causality principle look like?

We can certainly think of many events in the past for which we never *discovered* the cause; and we can imagine events happening for which we might never *find* the cause. But what do we conclude in either of these cases? That there is no cause? Or simply that the cause has evaded or will somehow evade us?

Suppose, to take an example within science, that we were chemists charged with investigating the properties of the organic substance called vinyl chloride. And suppose — what is of course very far from the case — that this is a substance of which we are very ignorant, and in particular imagine that we do not know what it is that makes the small molecules of vinyl chloride link up to form the long-chain molecules of *poly*vinyl chloride. Sometimes, let us suppose, we find it in the 'monomer' state, with all the molecules separate; and some- times we find it as a polymer, with the molecules linked up. And suppose we set ourselves the problem: what conditions are necessary for the monomers to link up — that is, for it to polymerize?

The first thing we think of might be *heat*. Perhaps the substance polymerizes if subjected to a certain critical temperature. We try this out in the laboratory: put some in a test-tube, raise its temperature and see whether polymerization occurs.

Let us suppose that in fact it *does* polymerize. Then suppose that we are cautious persons — perhaps overcautious — and that we go through the procedure once again in order to make sure. But on this second occasion to our surprise nothing happens. The vinyl chloride, in spite of being heated, refuses to polymerize and remains as it is.

We have to conclude from this development that temperature cannot be the whole story. The fact that nothing happened on the second run means that some other factor must be involved, which was present during the first run, but absent during the second. So our business is to find that factor.

We might guess at degree of illumination. Perhaps by some accident there was more light shining on the test-tube the first time than in the second, and that *this* made the crucial difference. So we set up a light-tight room with controlled illumination and see if the substance polymerizes consistently when above or below a certain degree of illumination. Suppose we draw a blank. On some of the runs at a certain degree of illumination it polymerizes, but on some runs at the same illumination it does not.

So we have to think of other possible factors. Can it be accidental electrical fields that are causing these unhelpful results, or magnetic fields? Or is it the catalytic action of an impurity sometimes present in the test-tube glass? Can it be slight variations in air pressure? One by one we try out these possibilities and get nowhere. We can find no consistent correlation between the substance polymerizing and the operation of any one of these factors.

Reluctantly, because we can see an enormous amount of work ahead of us, we begin to think of *combinations*. Perhaps the crucial factor is, for example, neither heat alone nor light alone but both *combined*. So we try this. And draw a blank. And then we try the other possible combinations. And continue to draw a blank.

Hypotheses of this kind are of course numberless, and we could go on for ever putting them forward and then to the test. We could go on searching for the cause of polymerization, that is to say, indefinitely; and the question we must ask is whether we would be right at any stage to conclude that further search was pointless since we must be dealing with a phenomenon that *has no cause*. Of course, we might very well give up the attempt to *find* the cause as too difficult and too time-consuming. But would we ever be driven to the conclusion that there *was* no cause? — that this is a substance that polymerizes 'spontaneously', as it were, without anything whatever bringing it about?

It is at least tempting to think that this is a conclusion we could never be *forced* to accept; for whatever happened it would be open to us to point out that there were an indefinite number of possibilities not yet checked through, or to invoke the limitations of existing knowledge and human imagination: maybe, we could suggest, the cause is something of which we have no inkling in the present state of science.

Our worried response to alleged 'inexplicable' occurrences is witness, it might be argued, to our commitment at a deep, not very conscious level, to the principle of causality. If the alarm clock on my mantelshelf for no apparent reason suddenly flies across the room I shall not find it calming to be told that I have simply observed an event without a cause. I shall surely feel very strongly that *something* must have caused it, and if I can't discover any physical cause I shall in a disturbed way begin to think of forces that physics doesn't recognize; or, even more disturbed, of causes that belong to the supernatural. In the past, at least — as recently as the nineteenth century — it was indeed common to take it that if one could demonstrate the occurrence of phenomena like telepathy and levitation, for which science could not give a causal explanation, one had a powerful argument for the existence of the supernatural. For, it was assumed, *something* must bring these effects to pass, and, if the cause was not in nature, it must be beyond.

Our commitment to the principle of causality, then, certainly seems to run deep; and to the extent that it does so we have an example of a belief belonging to our Western scientific conceptual framework that we protect from the criticism of experience.

Before overemphasizing the point, however, we must take account of the claim that as a matter of historical fact the experience of scientists in the field of physics during the early part of this century *did* oblige them to give up the principle under discussion. Sustained experimental work and theorizing led to the gradual acceptance of an approach which postulated the *causeless* occurrence of certain events at the level of atomic structure, and so the abandonment of the causality principle. We cannot, I think, take this fascinating development any further here, but it clearly sounds a warning against the argument I have been trying to present that in the causality principle we have a thoroughly unfalsifiable belief.

4 *Concluding remarks*

I cannot claim, therefore, to have given a clear example of a principle belonging to our own world-view which is completely invulnerable to experience. What I hope has emerged as plausible, however, is the idea that some conceptions are not as easily check-able as may at first appear. The Azande belief in the efficacy of soil fertility rites and our (layman's) belief (which the Azande share, incidentally) in the principle of causality are not beliefs that a few carefully thought-out and well-conducted experiments or observations could show to be correct or false. They are more like assumptions with which we approach our empirical work than results derived from it: more like preconceptions than conclusions.

8 Explanation and prediction

1 Introduction

We have in the last three chapters discussed a number of ways in which conceptual thought may be held to 'structure' our experience. Some of these ways apply, if at all, to our experience of both natural and social worlds without distinction. But *one* way, explored by Peter Winch, for example, applies (if at all) to the world of human beings alone. It insists that human behaviour, as distinct from the behaviour of inanimate things, is *meaningful*, with the clear implication that there must be a big difference between studying human beings and studying the world of inanimate nature. Those who stress the meaningful character of human behaviour, in other words, are generally opposed to the assimilation of social study by natural science.

But to say as much is unfortunately to be rather unspecific, since people do not agree on the nature of natural science itself. Some of these disagreements we shall have to enter in on as we pursue an understanding of the conflict between 'scientistic' and 'anti-scientistic' conceptions of social study — the conflict which in fact separates students of society into two mutually unsympathetic camps.

2 The 'covering-law' thesis

A thesis about scientific explanation that has been very influential in recent thought, and which 'anti-scientistic' students of society would wish to reject, is known as the 'deductive-nomological' model of explanation or as the 'covering-law' thesis. This was developed by two American philosophers, C. G. Hempel and P. Oppenheim.

It holds that a scientific explanation (in order to be genuine) must have three types of component. First, it must incorporate one or more general principles or laws; second, there must be some statement of a particular fact or facts; and, third, there must be a statement describing whatever it is that is being explained. What the explanation does is to show that the thing to be explained follows from the general principles, given that the particular facts also hold.

Take my explanation of the fact that the light in the kitchen has gone out: a fuse has blown. Although I don't say so explicitly, this claim only acts as an explanation if the general principles that, whenever the fuse of a circuit blows, the current is interrupted, and that whenever the current is interrupted the light fails are taken as understood. When we formulate these principles explicitly and add to them the statement of particular fact that I cited — that the fuse has blown — a statement describing the fact to be explained can be seen *to follow by logic*. We can draw up the relationship as follows:

> *Premiss 1*   Whenever the fuse in a lighting circuit blows, the current is interrupted.
>
> *Premiss 2*   Whenever the current in a lighting circuit is interrupted, the light fails.
>
> *Premiss 3*   The fuse in this particular lighting circuit has blown.
>
> *Therefore:*
> *Conclusion*   This particular light has failed.

With the exception of probabilistic explanations, to which I shall refer in a moment, all genuine scientific explanations can be formulated so as to conform to the same pattern, it is claimed. Each is essentially an argument, in which the thing to be explained is deduced from premisses, of which there must be two kinds: one stating a universal law or laws; the other stating a particular fact or facts.

3   *The 'probabilistic' modification*

In 'probabilistic' explanations, it is held, the pattern is modified, but only slightly. 'Laws' still figure, but they are statistical in character, asserting not what *always* happens in certain circumstances but what *very often* happens. When, for example, I account for the fact that Sophie has caught mumps by referring to the fact that some days ago she came into contact with Tom, who was already down with it, I am appealing to the 'probabilistic law' that people exposed to mumps *very often* catch it. Because the law is not a universal one, the thing to be explained does not in these cases actually follow deductively from the law(s) and fact(s) adduced. But these law(s) and fact(s) *do* make the thing to be explained 'more probable'. The structure of such probabilistic explanations can be expressed as follows:

Premiss 1   The percentage of people catching mumps after contact with someone who has it is high.

Premiss 2   Sophie was in contact with someone who had it.

Therefore it is probable that:

Conclusion   Sophie caught mumps.

4 *Pyramidal structure of science*

The generality of the claim that the deductive-nomological pattern (including the 'probabilistic' modification) is followed by every genuine scientific explanation generates a distinctive view of the nature of science as a whole. To explain events, it argues, we seek laws under which to subsume them. But then, as science advances, we shall seek explanations of those laws themselves: *why* is mumps catching? *why* does interrupting the current cause the tungsten to stop glowing? With the covering-law thesis the only way of explaining such laws is to put forward further laws of wider generality, so that several low-level laws are subsumed under a higher-level law — the contagiousness of measles, chicken pox and whooping cough as well as mumps may be explained by reference to a law stating that pathogens are transferred by bodily contact. These wider laws will themselves come under investigation in due course. What explains *these*? And once again the covering-law thesis will insist that the only way to pursue the question will be to seek *more* laws — of still greater generality.

Science is thus seen as engaged in building a kind of pyramid. At the bottom are descriptions of particular happenings, forming an extremely broad base. At the top will be a law of perfect generality. In the middle, laws of intermediate scope, which widens as the pyramid is ascended.

At the moment, perhaps, the structure is far from complete, but the ultimate object is clear: the formulation of a single grand law which covers *everything*, a law from which all lesser laws may be deduced and in terms of which *everything* that happens may be understood.

5 *Prediction*

The pyramidal conception of scientific knowledge is thus one implication of the 'covering-law' thesis concerning the logical structure of explanation. A second concerns prediction.

Later we shall consider more fully the relation between *explaining* a thing and being able to *predict* it, but here we may notice that the covering-law thesis takes it to be a relation that is very close indeed. For if an event is explained only when you show that its occurrence can be deduced from certain premisses, it follows that knowing the premisses before the event happened would have enabled you to have predicted that it would happen.

In the above example we explain the sudden blackness by reference to laws asserting that for an electric bulb to be illuminated it must belong to a completed electrical circuit, which the blowing of a fuse interrupts. It seems clear in this case that, if we had known of these laws before the lamp went out and had known that the fuse was about to blow, we could have *predicted* the blackout.

The thesis that declares all true explanations to exhibit this 'deductive-nomological' pattern obviously implies that they all have the same intimate connection with prediction: known beforehand, they would have allowed the occurrence in question to have been predicted.

6 *Social study and general laws*

The anti-scientistic case against the covering-law thesis is that although *natural* science may indeed be concerned to establish the general laws which any explanation of the covering-law pattern requires, social study has different concerns.

It is true that the mushrooming of social study over the last 100 or 150 years was partly inspired by the notion that social study *was* a matter of searching for general laws. The hope was that the methods that had helped natural science to enjoy so much success in establishing laws could simply be transferred to the study of people and society. But was that hope well founded? Perhaps it should not have been assumed that explanation in the social sphere has the same structure as in natural science. Perhaps general laws are required only by the latter.

At least it seems, so it is argued, that general laws play no part in many ordinary explanations of human behaviour. Suppose I account for my action in striding out of a lecture by explaining that I had been outraged by the lecturer's contempt for certain political views that I held. Here we have, surely, an acceptable explanation of a piece of conduct. But does it refer to a general law?

Perhaps, it may be said, the explanation is implicitly appealing to the general law that *people in lectures walk out when their political sensibilities are outraged?* But then the explanation would have to be rejected as unacceptable, since this 'general law' does not hold. It may be that many people walk out when offended in this way, but surely many do not: they may shout their protests, or simply sit still, coldly furious.

A second suggestion might be that the law involved concerns not everybody but people with a given character or disposition. Everyone with my particular temperament, such a law might run, walks out of a lecture which has insulted their political beliefs.

But people often act 'out of character'. It may easily be, in this particular case, that I was doing something especially extrovert by the standards of my own usual behaviour. Normally, it may be, I am the type of person simply to go on sitting there feeling frustrated; it was just *this* time that from somewhere I found the courage actually to demonstrate my feelings.

Parallel objections, it is argued, will apply to *any* general statement that is put forward as the 'law' to which my explanation is supposed to appeal; and in fact, it is claimed, no such law exists. What I am doing in putting my explanation forward is to indicate the *reason* for my action, and this has nothing to do with general laws.

7 Social study as yielding control

Associated with the applicability of the covering-law model of explanation is a conception of the nature of the scientific enterprise as a whole. When a scientist puts forward an explanation following the covering-law pattern, he has before him the phenomenon to be explained; and, in conjunction with a statement of the conditions that obtain, he uses a general law to *explain* what has happened. Under different circumstances, however, it may be that we are interested not so much in explaining a phenomenon that has already occurred, but in *knowing what to expect* in the future. A general law may again be of use; for if we take it in conjunction with a knowledge of what conditions are likely to prevail it will allow us to deduce what will happen.

It is this second application of general laws that leads to a distinctively 'utilitarian' conception of science. It is easy to assume — perhaps it is assumed in what I have written so far — that science's endeavour is to increase man's understanding, to provide explanations for what he can observe happening in the universe about him. According to the type of view we are now considering, such a view is not so much wrong as radically incomplete, for it leaves out of account the crucial matter of *why* such a search for understanding takes place. The truth is that man seeks to understand what happens in the world about him not out of idle curiosity — not simply because, as the historian of science Charles Singer colourfully puts it, 'there is an unquenchable and irresistible thirst of the soul that demands an explanation of the world in which it finds itself' — *but in order to strengthen his grasp on his own future*. The enterprise of science represents in short man's attempt to control his environment.

8 *Predictive power*

Science's contribution to control lies, as we have said, in the predictive capacity of its general laws. They enable one to know what will happen under specified conditions, so that what is not wanted can be avoided by ensuring that the necessary conditions do not arise, and what *is* wanted may be brought on, in this case by making sure that the necessary circumstances *do* come about. People who take this view — 'positivists' is a convenient label — may accordingly be found placing all their emphasis on the predictive aspect of scientific theorizing. 'The ultimate goal of a positive science', writes the contemporary economist Milton Friedman, 'is the development of a "theory" or "hypothesis" that yields valid and meaningful (i.e. not truistic) predictions about phenomena not yet observed.'

This conception of science has a number of interesting implications, of which I shall outline just one: it has led some thinkers to argue, against one's intuitions, perhaps, that there is no need for a theory to be based upon assumptions which are true to reality.

9 *'Realism' of theoretical assumptions*

Often in developing theories, both in natural science and social study, certain assumptions are made about the object of study. We have referred more than once to the kinetic theory of gases, which at any rate *began* by making the assumption that gases were made up of invisibly small particles rushing about in cheerful abandon; and economics is usually seen as basing itself on assumptions about human behaviour, for example, that 'individuals can arrange their preferences in an order' (Lionel Robbins) or that man's behaviour 'displays the characteristic of seeking to have more' (an economics textbook).

At first blush we might easily think that, if such theorizing is to stand a chance of being valid, the assumptions it makes must be true. If, for example, we were to develop a theory of the apparent motions of the heavenly bodies on the assumption that the earth is at the centre of the universe, it would, we shall surely say, be bound to be wrong. A secure building just cannot be erected on foundations that are faulty.

An important implication of positivism as we are understanding it here is brought out by the fact that it rejects this apparently straightforward attitude towards assumptions. What is crucial about a theory, it reiterates, are its *predictive* powers: accept this point and it will be seen that the truth of a theory's assumptions should not enter into the assessment of its value. Whether it generates accurate predictions will then be seen as the only relevant issue.

It has been argued, indeed, that truth in assumptions actually *gets in the way* of predictive capacity, the point being, I think (though not to my mind a valid one), that efficient prediction depends on simplifying the full complexity of reality, and simplifying is a form of falsifying. Friedman at any rate arrives at this conclusion:

> Truly important and significant hypotheses will be found to have 'assumptions' that are wildly inaccurate descriptive representations of reality, and, in general, the more significant the theory, the more unrealistic the assumptions (in this sense) ... the relevant question to ask about the 'assumptions' of a theory is not whether they are descriptively 'realistic', for they never are, but whether they are sufficiently good approximations for the purpose in hand. And this question can be answered only by seeing whether the theory works, which means whether it yields sufficiently accurate predictions.

The interesting case of Ptolemaic astronomy perhaps gives a more concrete sense of what is being argued here. Publishing his extraordinarily influential compendium *Almagest* in the second century AD, the Egyptian astronomer Ptolemy spoke of heavenly bodies moving round each other in a variety of ways, some of them complex. Some planets were treated as going round the earth, for example, but with a centre of rotation near but not quite coincident with it; in the case of others, this point of rotation was itself supposed to orbit the earth; while in other cases again the centre of rotation was supposed to be far distant from the earth, again itself orbiting the latter. A superficial reading might suggest that Ptolemy is attempting to put forward in this highly complex picture of heavenly movements a theory as to where the bodies in the universe were actually located and how they actually moved. But in fact his 'constructions' were meant merely as *devices for predicting* the observable heavenly phenomena. To provide a rule by which the observed movements across the sky of the different bodies could be predicted, Ptolemy proposed that we think of them *as if* moving in the ways I have illustrated. But he did not mean to suggest that they were so related in actual fact. Indeed, they couldn't be, since some of his constructions are mutually incompatible. He was engaged not in trying to describe the universe but in elaborating a *calculating device* with the use of which astronomical prediction could be reliably made.

In Ptolemaic astronomy, then, we have a historical case of a 'theory' that was acknowledged to be based on factually false assumptions and yet was valued nevertheless for its predictive power. Friedman and those who think like him seem to suggest that Ptolemy should be emulated by theorizers in general: a recommendation that I have suggested arises naturally out of stressing the importance of the predictive aspect of a theory.

9 Explanation and understanding

1 *Introduction*

If it is held that explanation in the human sphere is *not* a matter of finding 'covering laws', what different conception of it might there be?

One line of thought which links with our earlier discussion of 'meaningfulness' begins with the idea that what an explanation must do is to provide *understanding*. Something happens which puzzles us, and in seeking an explanation we are seeking to understand it. This can only be, it is suggested, by assimilating what we cannot understand to what we *can* — by showing that things that puzzle us are capable of being interpreted, in some not immediately obvious way, as 'the same' as things that do *not* puzzle us.

2 *R. D. Laing*

The interesting writings of R. D. Laing may be taken to appeal to this idea. He considers the prima facie baffling behaviour we identify as 'schizophrenic' and tries to display it as after all intelligible, once one takes full account of the schizophrenic's experience and standpoint.

In *The Divided Self* Laing discusses, for example, the account given by Kraepelin at the beginning of the century of a patient said to be in a state of catatonic excitement brought for demonstration purposes in front of a class of students. When asked where he is, according to Kraepelin's account, the patient says: 'You want to know that too? I tell you who is being measured and is measured and shall be measured. I know all that, and could tell you, but I do not want to.'

To Kraepelin, this outburst is so much nonsense. It does not convey, he says, 'a single piece of useful information'; it consists only of 'a series of disconnected sentences having no relation whatever to the general situation.'

Laing, on the other hand, tries to show that the patient's remarks and generally hostile, uncooperative demeanour appear as intelligible when considered against the background of his situation. Presumably, says Laing, 'he deeply resents this form of interrogation which is being carried out before a lecture-room of students. He probably does not see what it has to do with the things that must be deeply distressing him.' When we ask in this light what the patient is saying we shall see that he is surely 'carrying on a dialogue between his own parodied version of Kraepelin and his own defiant rebelling self.' Then, his outburst 'seems to be plain enough talk'.

3 *Freud*

An even more important figure who can be interpreted as having the same orientation towards psychological explanation, at least some of the time, is Sigmund Freud.

Take, for example, the obsessional routine engaged in by one of Freud's most well-known patients, the 'Rat Man', which involved the patient's ensuring that he was studying late into the night. Between midnight and one o'clock he would put his book down and go to the door as if to let someone in. He would then switch on all the lights he could, strip, and display his penis in front of a mirror.

Here, on the face of it, we have a series of actions that are unintelligible. Freud, however, sees them as giving expression to his relationship with his father, his desire to impress him with his industry, which is the role of the first part of the routine (representing the father catching him working late), and his wish to defy him, which is the role of the second, (according to Freud) quasi-masturbating, part.

How exactly do these explanations of Freud's work? How do they illuminate or make intelligible the Rat Man's apparently nonsensical routine? A number of different answers have been given, but one possibility is that Freud is placing the unintelligible behaviour alongside actions we *can* understand, and assimilating one to the other by asserting crucial correspondences. Alongside the 'patient's' show of reading late into the night and his play of opening the door and letting someone in, Freud places the idea of a boy trying to impress his father. Alongside the patient's displaying nude in front of a mirror and subjecting his penis to scrutiny, Freud places the idea of a boy defying his father. Freud would then be assuming that our doing things to impress our father, or to confront him with defiance, is straightforwardly understandable, and the explanation lies in assimilating to such behaviour actions that are not so straightforward.

Both these writers, then, seem to be appealing to the idea that some of the things men do we can understand straight away, but that other things we cannot. This, however, only raises the basic question: what is it about an immediately intelligible action that *makes* it intelligible?

4 *The intelligibility of actions*

The philosopher Frank Cioffi makes one approach to this question in referring to the writings of Thorstein Veblen. Veblen, as a sociologist, attempts to throw light on the phenomenon that has come to be called 'conspicuous consumption' — crudely, the fact that people often like to spend money in ways that make it plain that they have money to spend (on spectacular parties, for example). Cioffi's charge is that this is an absurd endeavour, since this feature of human behaviour is entirely familiar to us. How can we understand it more than we do already? Veblen's attempt is to explain what needs no explanation.

Cioffi, then, is perhaps suggesting that it is the *familiarity* of an action or type of action which makes it intelligible and thus renders sociological explanation of it inappropriate. The action of a man donning an overcoat before going out into a storm is one with which we are entirely familiar, whereas the behaviour of a person who lies down in the middle of the road is strange, and therefore needs explaining.

The notion of 'familiarity', however, is perhaps not entirely unambiguous. One way in which we might be familiar with an action is by having frequently encountered it. But another sort of familiarity is the familiarity that comes from having performed the action ourselves.

The special feature of this second kind of familiarity is that when an action is our own we know that it is associated with a particular kind of 'conscious experience'. When I throw the clock I am trying to mend across the room, for example, I know that what I am doing is a manifestation of an irrepressible feeling of frustration welling up within me. When I stand stock still for 30 minutes at the side of a busy road as the rain pours down I know that the 'inner experience' which my behaviour manifests is the hope of a bus.

It is this familiarity-from-the-inside, so some have argued, that constitutes 'intelligibility' as far as actions are concerned. What I understand immediately, what it makes no sense to seek to explain, are actions of the kind I myself have performed, for in their case I know the 'inner experience' with which they are associated. Understanding other people's behaviour is thus a matter of interpreting it as somehow involving those same associations, and can only be achieved 'by reconstituting our own inner experience "in" the other person by "reading" him' (G. Walsh). This approach to explanation in social science is associated with the name of Wilhelm Dilthey and more generally with the anti-positivist tradition of which the sociologist Max Weber is an even more eminent representative. We shall return to it in more detail later. For the present let it stand as an example of how the thesis that explaining is a matter of assimilating the unintelligible to the intelligible might apply in the social sphere. Some actions, it suggests, do not stand in need of explanation: they are in some sense 'transparent' or understandable directly. And it is in terms of these actions that all the rest must be understood.

5 One use of models

The general conception of explanation involved here enables us to understand one aspect of the familiar scientific practice of developing what are called 'models'. For, at least in one sense of the term, in offering a *model* of a hitherto unexplained phenomenon, one is putting forward an already intelligible phenomenon and, by suggesting an analogy between the two, proposing to assimilate the unintelligible to the intelligible.

In his 'Field Theory' of human behaviour, for example, the twentieth-century psychologist Kurt Lewin suggested that the individual person was to be thought of as a body situated in a field of force. We understand that a magnet, say, situated in the region of a number of other magnets, will come under the influence of a variety of forces, pulling and pushing in a variety of directions. Whether it moves, in what direction and with what acceleration will depend on the interplay of these forces, and on the presence of any physical obstructions in the neighbourhood. A person, suggests Lewin, may be thought of analogously. The 'field of force' surrounding him will then be taken as being produced by the goals the person wishes to attain, and by the circumstances he wishes to avoid. Each goal and 'anti-goal' is thought (on the model) to exert a force, attractive or repulsive as the case may be, and the person is thought of as moving in the direction indicated by the resultant of these forces. In addition, something in a person's environment preventing him from reaching a goal is represented as a physical barrier interposed between the body and the source of attraction towards which it would otherwise move.

Thus the model is proposed. On the one hand there is human behaviour as it occurs in real life, and on the other a physical object subject to a variety of physical forces. The assumption is, I think it is clear, that the behaviour of a body under the influence of physical forces is intelligible and that of a human being less so. The physicist and indeed the rest of us are reasonably familiar with the notion of a body pulled this way and that by the play of various conflicting forces; and we understand without difficulty the effect of blocking the path of a physical object with a physical barrier. But human behaviour, Lewin's treatment implies, is more puzzling. Why did Tom do this? Why didn't Dick do that? Why is Harry doing the other? By proposing the model an offer is made to dispel the bafflement. Imagine that Tom, Dick and Harry are physical objects, he says, being pulled by positive forces, pushed by negative ones. All that is necessary is for the details of this analogy to be worked out, and the behaviour of the human being, 'seen as' the behaviour of a physical object, then becomes intelligible.

Those who conceive of explanation as the assimilation of the prima facie unintelligible to the intelligible are bound to lay great stress on models, for their view amounts to an assertion that it is in fact a *model* that any explanatory theory must provide: its very point will be the striking of an analogy between what is to be understood and what is understood already.

10 Acquiring scientific knowledge

1 Introduction

One issue separating those who see social study as a branch of science and those who see it as a distinctive study of *meaningful* behaviour is thus what counts as an explanation in the human sphere. A second, perhaps obviously enough, is how to go about establishing such explanations as it is appropriate to seek.

2 Inductivism

In so far as science seeks to establish general laws, it might seem that the most straightforward way for it to proceed would be to make a great number of observations and see what general laws those particular observations added up to.

Schematically, if we represent the various facts that have been established as *a, b, c, d,* etc., and if we write T for the theory that is supposed to come from them, we may express the alleged relationship between the facts and the theory like this:

a is a fact
b is a fact
c is a fact
d is a fact
.
.
.

therefore, T is a valid theory.

The theory is supposed to follow from the facts by a rigorous process of argument.

This conception of how scientific theories are established is sometimes called *inductivism*, and, though it may seem reasonable at first sight, it is in fact open to a number of serious objections. The most relevant of these from our point of view raises 'the problem of induction'. It argues that no *general* theory can be properly substantiated by any series of particular facts, no matter how long.

Let us take a very simple case of a general claim and see how it might be related to relevant particular facts: all human beings raise their eyebrows for a split second when meeting a stranger. We may imagine that anthropologists have observed a great many cases of the 'eyebrow flash' as it is called, and have drawn this general conclusion on that basis. Our question is: were they right to do so? Does it follow from the fact that very many people exhibit the eyebrow flash that *all* of them do so? Surely, it is tempting to admit, not with absolute rigour. The conclusion asserts something that we have not actually checked up on, and as such cannot be stated with certainty, even if the many particular facts cited are accepted. There *may* be an odd person out, or even several. We can't really know that there will be no exceptions, no matter how many positive instances have been observed.

Perhaps we shall be tempted to insist, however, that the general conclusion must be likely to be true, and moreover that the more individual cases are observed, the more likely to be true it becomes.

It is at this point that the 'problem of induction' begins to bewilder. For it suggests that this tolerant concession does not go far enough. The 'problem of induction' suggests that the accumulation of positive cases does nothing to make the conclusion likely, and that in fact the argument from them to it is no argument at all.

What principle, we have to ask ourselves, allows us to think that cases we have *not* observed will be similar to cases we *have*? What principle allows us to think that the encounters between strangers at which we have actually looked will resemble those we have never seen?

An attempt at an answer might begin: surely we must accept the principle that all encounters between strangers resemble each other in all important respects? Our observation of a 'representative' number will then indeed justify our general claim. But if a principle like this is appealed to, the question inevitably arises of how it could be established. It is *another* general principle, and all that we should be able to say in its defence is that in all the cases studied so far encounters between strangers resemble each other. But then the same question arises as before: what gives us the right to think that *unobserved* cases will be like *observed* ones? We have made no progress. With only uninteresting exceptions, which we shall note in a moment, *wherever* there is a general principle the same problem can be raised. The principle can only be supported, presumably, by an appeal to *particular facts* — even though there may be a great number of them. But in going beyond the particular facts to a general assertion we must surely appeal to a principle which justifies the step. Such a principle will itself be general, however, and will itself only be justifiable by an appeal to a different set of particular facts taken in conjunction with a *further* principle which allows us to generalize from them.

One simplified way of expressing the problem is to say that general principles are of the form *All As are Bs*. It is true that in some cases it would be possible to check literally every A and thus demonstrate the truth of the general principle by what William Kneale calls *complete enumeration*. We could show, for example, that all the swans in Kelling Park Aviary were white by calling in at the aviary and inspecting each and every individual swan there. The general propositions of interest to science, however, refer to things belonging to classes that are indefinitely large. The claim that *All swans whatever are white*, for example, refers to swans that are yet to be conceived and hatched as well as to past and contemporary individuals, so that their number is not definite. *All iron is magnetic* again refers to the iron that has yet to be extracted from its ores as well as to iron that is or has been in existence, and so refers to a category that is not finite.

With universal claims of this type — claims of 'unrestricted universality' as they are sometimes called — there is no possibility of establishing them by checking each individual case. All we can establish is a proposition of the form 'Some As are Bs'. The problem of induction can then be put by asking how we can ever be justified in thinking that our findings about some individuals can be generalized to apply to *all*.

3 *Hypothetico-deductivism*

The problem of induction is just one of the difficulties which have led people to look for a better account of how scientific theories are arrived at. 'Hypothetico-deductivism' is the rebarbative title by which one such alternative, a very influential one, is known. We have seen difficulties, it is said, in any attempt to show a theory to be true — the difficulties that make inductivism unacceptable to many.

What is infinitely more straightforward, it is then suggested, is show-ing a theory to be *false* — for all that is necessary is to find a particu-lar instance that runs counter to it. For example, the theory proposed by the seventeenth-century philosopher Thomas Hobbes — that 'of the voluntary acts of every man, the object is some *good to himself'* — cannot be maintained in the face of even one case of a man doing something unselfishly; and the sociological thesis that all societies have rules of some kind governing sexual relationships must be discarded once a single society is brought forward which can be shown to lack such arrangements. Science, it is said, capitalizes on this helpful logical situation. It proceeds not by trying to arrive at theories on the basis of 'induction' from the observations, but by using its observations to disprove theories. Where scientists obtain their theories, or how, doesn't matter. What matters is that they should be tested by checking them against observed fact, and dis-carded the moment a 'counter-instance' is discovered.

The scientist begins, therefore, by putting forward a 'hypothesis'; then he deduces from it something that should be observable if it were true; and by carrying out observations he goes on to check whether this prediction is fulfilled. If it is not, the hypothesis must be discarded. The only option is to try to think of a new hypothesis and to subject *that* to tests. If, on the other hand, the prediction is ful-filled, the hypothesis remains unfalsified and so may be retained.

The rejection of the theory of 'phlogiston' might be given by 'hypothetico-deductivists' as exemplifying their account. Asserting that the process of burning consisted in the giving off of a substance, phlogiston, the theory implied that a lump of metal should weigh less after being burnt that it did before. But (it might be claimed) Lavoisier showed that in fact burning involves a *gain* in weight, and so the phlogiston theory had to be abandoned.

For a case that might be held to exemplify the hypothetico-deductive method resulting in a hypothesis being retained, one might quite arbitrarily cite Durkheim's study of *Suicide*. According to at least one interpretation of this work, he advances the theory that belonging to tightly knit groups helps to improve people's resistance to stress.

Since social groupings united by Catholic Christianity tend to be more cohesive than those of the Protestant faith, argues Durkheim, one may deduce that stress is likely to do more damage in Protestant communities; and one way of measuring stress is to consult suicide rates. With these auxiliary assumptions, therefore, Durkheim's theory yields a testable prediction — that suicide rates are likely to be higher in Protestant communities than they are in Catholic communities, other things being equal. Accordingly he gathers relevant statistical evidence of suicide rates to show that the prediction of his theory is indeed borne out by the facts, and that it therefore stands.

4 *Science as guessing*

Science thus proceeds according to hypothetico-deductivism by taking hypotheses, no matter how arrived at, deducing predictions from them and seeing whether these predictions are fulfilled in reality.

But this 'whether' hides an embarrassment. If a theory's predictions are falsified by reality, then it certainly seems plausible to think that the theory is thereby discredited. But what is the position if the predictions are fulfilled? It is tempting to say that in this case the theory is *supported*: the more tests a theory passes successfully, surely, the more established it becomes. There are many writers, it is true, who find themselves able to yield to this temptation. But they are able to do so only because they do not fully accept the arguments that we presented as leading to hypothetico-deductivism. In particular, they can do so only if they reject the arguments against the possibility of *induction*. For when a hypothesis 'passes a test' all that can be said is that a fact has been discovered with which the general proposition (the hypothesis) is compatible. Does such a fact *support* the general proposition? If we said that it did, we should be acknowledging the validity of an *inductive* argument — we should be admitting that a particular fact can help to verify a general proposition (the hypothesis). Only for those who believe in the possibility of induction, therefore, is it possible to think of hypotheses as becoming gradually stronger as they pass successive tests. For those who embrace hypothetico-deductivism partly because they reject the possibility of induction, the notion of hypotheses becoming 'better established' — the notion of 'evidence building up' for a particular theory — is completely invalid. Hypotheses that survive tests survive, but that is all. They are no better established for their ordeal; so that a hypothesis or theory may have been subjected to a series of tests extending over decades or even centuries, and have passed them all, yet it would, on a view which rejected the possibility of induction, remain absolutely unsupported by evidence. Its long history of escaping failure in the past makes it not one whit more likely to escape disproof in the future: that is the consequence of accepting the invalidity of induction. 'All our theories', says the leading exponent of a version of this view, the contemporary philosopher

Karl Popper, 'remain guesses, conjectures, hypotheses'; so that in this respect there is no difference between the suggestion that the earth goes round the sun and the latest brainchild of the theoretical physicist.

In spite of this implication, which certainly seems paradoxical to some, hypothetico-deductivism has been and remains probably the most widely held account of how scientific thought develops; and it is this conception of scientific procedure that, I think it is true to say, anti-scientistic students of human affairs are particularly keen to reject. The study of people, in their view, cannot properly consist of putting forward hypotheses and then subjecting them to observational or experimental tests.

5 Anti-scientistic approaches

But what alternative methods of study might be suggested? Different anti-scientistic thinkers make different suggestions.

We have already seen in an earlier section, to take one example, how those whose approach to meaningful behaviour is to place the *intention* associated with an action in the centre of the stage may be led to insist that the explanations proper to it are not of the covering-law pattern. The associated conception of the method of study appropriate to human affairs stresses the role of the imagination. One is to achieve an understanding of another person's behaviour by feeling one's way into one's subject's skin, by sharing in imagination their feelings and beliefs. Only once we are in a position to say we 'know how it feels', it is asserted, shall we be able to recognize their motives, the reasons which count for them, the things they think important and those they neglect; only then shall we come to understand the springs of their action. One is tempted to say that the activity of the student of social life on this view becomes that of the novelist or, perhaps better, the *biographer*.

The thought of the twentieth-century philosopher R. G. Collingwood exemplifies this approach to the study of human behaviour, at least as regards historical inquiry: 'For science, the event is discovered by perceiving it, and the further search for its cause is conducted by assigning it to its class and determining the relation between that class and others. For history, the object to be discovered is not the mere event, but the thought expressed in it.' In attempting to understand the behaviour of a historical figure, the historian, according to Collingwood, has to work out what considerations entered into the decision that lay behind the action. He has to look at the world from his subject's point of view — to 're-enact' the thinking that his subject must have engaged in; and when (as a commentator, W. Dray, puts it) he can see that the subject's 'beliefs, purposes, principles, etc., give him a reason for doing what he did, then he can claim to understand the action'.

In putting the emphasis elsewhere, not on the conscious considering which may precede an action but on the rule followed in the performance of it, Winch puts forward alternative ideas about how social study should be conducted — though they are ideas that are not easy to fit together into a clear overall picture. For example, he attacks Weber for maintaining that empirically established causal laws have an essential role to play (alongside the appreciation of 'meanings') and almost leaves it open for the reader to conclude that he is advocating a sociology which does away with empirical research altogether.

Mistaken though this extreme construal of Winch may be, it is true, of course, that the effect of his thesis that actions are essentially rule-guided is to emphasize the role of 'conceptual' or 'quasi-conceptual' inquiry in social study at the expense of the purely empirical. Let me try to clarify just one way in which this bears on actual practice.

Before items of any kind can be 'explained' — or figure in talk of any kind — they have to be *identified*: I can't 'explain' what it is that the man outside on the pavement is doing without *saying* what it is that he is doing. In some circumstances, saying what he is doing will indeed constitute an 'explanation' in itself, as when I point out that he is waiting for a bus; but, whatever the case, *explanation* presupposes *identification*. If Winch is right about the nature of action this matter of identification will be a matter of discerning what rules the agent is following, rules that will in fact be embodied in the concept the agent has of his action. It will thus be quasi-linguistic — or, as we have said, *conceptual* in character.

Consider the case of a 'sociologist of religion' attempting to study prayer, for example, a case cited by Winch himself. Before offering any 'explanations', and even before conducting any empirical work, such an inquirer must try to establish what counts as the activity of 'praying'. And, unfortunately for his clarity of mind, he will of course realize that there are different answers to the question. In the gospel parable of the Pharisee and the Publican, for example, the Pharisee utters words that display deep pride and contempt for his fellow human beings, while the Publican speaks in humility of repentance. Are both to be regarded as 'praying'? Perhaps the gospel writer is himself suggesting that people can only enter into genuine prayer if they stop being arrogant and humbly seek forgiveness. The Pharisee, one must assume, would on the other hand not be prepared to accept this comment and would insist that his praying was as genuine as anyone's. In the face of such disagreements as these our sociologist must somehow decide what *he* is to regard as prayer; the suggestion is, as I have tried to explain, that this essential preliminary to any further inquiry is of a quasi-linguistic or 'conceptual' character.

Problems in identifying actions thus arise, it is said, even when the actions concerned take place in the context of the inquirer's own culture. But very much greater difficulties occur in attempts at inter-cultural study. The unfamiliar culture studied by the anthropologist, that is to say, may define actions in terms of quite different sets of rules from those recognized in the culture to which the anthropologist belongs; and correspondingly their concepts for actions may be quite different. Should one try to describe the activities of an unfamiliar people in terms of one's own concepts, misunderstanding is bound to result; and the only way to achieve a valid understanding, on this view, is for the anthropologist to 'learn the rules' that the people apply in their behaviour by sustained participation in their way of life.

These, then, are some of the points urged by those who insist on the distinctiveness and significance of the 'meaningfulness' of human activity. They constitute one very important kind of reason for denying that social study is a branch of natural science. Another kind of reason has been advanced, however, and that is the dimension of *value* within which human life is conducted. It is this that we consider next.

11 Social study and objectivity

1 Introduction

Human beings, it seems plausible to say, are typically subject to moral *obligations*, and this is a further difference between them and the objects studied by natural science.

It is widely thought, for example, that killing people needs justification, so that where there is no justification we have an obligation not to kill. Similarly, it is often held that one should not lie unless there is very special reason to do so; and that the well-fed and comfortable ought to show concern for the hungry and suffering. I imagine there would seem to be no difficulty in agreeing that these could all be categorized as *moral beliefs*: it is a category familiar to us, and ordinarily, most of the time, we surely have no difficulty in picking out those beliefs that belong to it and those that do not.

Trying to put one's finger on the distinctive character of such beliefs, however, is not easy.

2 The autonomy of values

An approach that has been deeply influential recently pursues the line of thought that is perhaps already begun in what I have said so far.

The crucial feature of a moral belief, it is said, is that it is a belief not about what the facts are but about how they *ought* to be. To say that we ought to do what we can for the hungry and suffering is not to say that as a matter of fact men *do* show such care; it is to say that we have an obligation to do so, that we are wrong or evil to behave indifferently.

The difference here is brought further into the open, it is said, when we ask about the logic of arguments in which moral beliefs figure. We then realize that judgements in morality can never be derived from purely factual premisses.

Suppose, for example, a girl was wondering whether to marry the boy she was living with; and suppose — perhaps it is a bizarre supposition — that one consideration was that her parents might not approve of her present way of life. Let us assume further that it is simply a fact of the situation that her parents *would* so disapprove. The question is then: would this fact in itself be an argument (not conclusive, perhaps) for marrying? We are invited to answer that it would *not*. The fact of parental disapproval is not a ground in itself for concluding that one ought to avoid what is so condemned; though that conclusion *would* be supported if there were added a further premiss expressing an appropriate 'moral judgement or belief', for example, that *one ought to avoid that which one's parents condemn*. Setting the argument out schematically:

Premiss 1   One's parents disapprove of extramarital sex.

Premiss 2   One ought to avoid that which one's parents disapprove of.

Therefore:

Conclusion   One ought to take steps to avoid extramarital sex (and so marry).

The point being made is that the conclusion, a matter of moral belief, does not follow from the first premiss alone (which states a matter of *fact*), though it does once there is added the second premiss, which is, like the conclusion, a statement about right and wrong.

Suppose, by way of a second example, that a student were urged to work for his exams on the grounds that if he should fail them he would be asked to leave college. This factual prediction the student might accept, agreeing that failure would lead to departure, and also that his present debauched style of life would certainly lead to failure; and yet he may combine these beliefs with the view that being expelled from college would be a highly valuable experience. He may believe that there could be no finer way of leaving college than by being sent away for protracted and incorrigible neglect of the academic round. *Ought* he to get down to some work therefore? From the facts alone we cannot tell. It depends on whether he 'values' his continuing college life. If it is his judgement that he ought to continue at college, then knowledge of the factual connection between work and continuance will lead him to conclude that he ought indeed to work. But a 'negative evaluation' of college life coupled with the same facts will lead elsewhere.

The thesis that these examples are meant to illustrate is that moral judgements cannot be deduced from factual statements alone, and that thesis in turn is taken to demonstrate what might be called a *logical* distinction between statements of moral judgement and statements of fact.

We have spoken so far of contrasting matters of fact with specifically *moral* judgements. Usually, however, those who defend the contrast I have been presenting locate moral judgements within the wider category of *value judgements*, and they thus make room for the possibility that some judgements about what *ought* to be may not belong to morality. For example, it is sometimes said that when a critic remarks of a painting that, say, *its composition ought to be stronger* he is making a 'value judgement' which is to do not with morality but with aesthetics. Similarly, it has been said that the obligation to obey the government (assuming that there is such an obligation) is not a moral obligation exactly but rather a *political* one.

In terms of this possibly wider category, then, what is being proposed is a dichotomy between matters of fact on the one hand, and matters of value on the other.

3   *Value judgements and arbitrariness*

The problem that this approach to morality encounters, however — or one of them — is that of giving an account of how value judgements are arrived at. The *facts* of a situation, we have just seen it argued, do not in themselves support any conclusion about what ought to be, or ought to be done. Such a conclusion follows only if a value judgement is added to the facts — and then the question is, where *that* value judgement originates. Value judgements, it seems, can only be derived on the basis of prior value judgements, so that the idea that we can test a moral belief of ours by looking simply to the facts, or that we can argue against a principle with which we disagree by citing merely factual evidence, is to be rejected.

Can we arrive at moral principles by the exercise of 'pure reason' unaided by any factual considerations? That is one avenue that has been explored. Another is the possibility that moral principles are somehow embedded in the structure of the universe and are discerned by a kind of sixth — or 'moral' — sense. But it is a third approach which has been of particular influence in recent moral philosophy and which correspondingly has played a major role in conceptions of the relationship between moral beliefs and social study. It is the idea that ultimately moral principles are things one simply *opts* for. They are incapable of being supported by factual evidence, they are not apprehended by any moral sense, and *a priori* reasoning is inappropriate.

In an act of selection which is worse than blind — for there is nothing there for a sighted man to see — one's moral principles are on this view simply *chosen*; though indeed it may be questioned whether the notion of *choice* makes sense in such a completely guideless situation. A man who declared that he happened to believe that all Jews ought to be murdered would thus, on this view, be doing no more than exercising his right to choose whatever moral principles he chose to choose! So long as he accepted all the logical implications of his principle, no factual evidence, no reasoning, could even tend to show that it was misguided. Others might happen to believe that killing people was wrong. So be it! As far as moral principles are concerned, one must simply take one's pick.

4 *Relativism*

The conception that is basic here — that no rational adjudication is possible between rival basic moral beliefs — is one that is arrived at by other thinkers following a different path.

They begin by drawing attention to the fact that people from different cultures often hold different moral beliefs. Eating what we should call other human beings is generally condemned in our culture, but has been thought quite permissible in certain circumstances by people of certain other cultures. The concept of an old people's home is acceptable here and now, but in some other cultures seems horrific. It is claimed that, though representatives of two cultures that differed in their moral beliefs might confront each other and might even appear to argue over their differences, these could never be rationally resolved.

A related point has been made in connection not with different cultures but with different 'moral traditions'. An example would be a 'disagreement' between someone belonging to the tradition of scientific rationalism and a Roman Catholic over birth control. The rationalist points to the injury to the mother's health that having many children often brings. But the Roman Catholic, on the other hand, speaks only of the 'honour' that a mother has in bringing children into the world.

It is not possible for real argument to take place between these two views, it is suggested, since they belong to different systems of belief. The appeal to the mother of 'honour' makes no sense to the rationalist: it is a concept that is foreign to his thought. For her it gives a reason for scorning birth control; for him it does not. How then can they ever enter into, let alone conclude, a genuine argument, when what counts as a reason for one counts as a meaningless irrelevance for the other? 'It is hard to see how they could', say the two writers who develop this example, 'without renouncing what they believe in.'

The point being argued is thus that we have difficulty in understanding how 'disputes' between different 'moral traditions' may be resolved. What they involve, it is claimed, is one person drawing on concepts which belong to *his* moral tradition, and appealing to reasons which make sense there, and the other speaking from a different moral tradition with its own, different, concepts, and its own different criteria for what is a good reason and what a bad.

Once again we arrive at the view that bringing forward evidence, adducing reasons, is of no relevance to the question of choosing between apparently rival moral beliefs. On the view just presented, it is true, reason may come into choosing between beliefs *within* a single 'tradition'; but when the question of which culture or 'tradition' is *right* about morality is raised, evidence and reasoning are held to be out of place.

As I have suggested, perhaps we can express the idea at the bottom of the approaches to morality so far discussed as the thesis that no rational adjudication is possible between rival basic moral beliefs of different people, particularly if they represent different cultures or 'traditions'. Its relevance to our particular interest in social study becomes clear when we place alongside it a further thesis that we have yet to explore: that no student of society can arrive at conclusions which are unaffected by his moral beliefs. Taken together, the two doctrines put a question mark against the whole point of bothering to try to conduct careful inquiries into the nature of man and society. For, if the inquirer's values are, in the sense we have discussed, 'arbitrary' and if they necessarily mould or condition the inquirer's conclusions, must we not accept that *they* will be uselessly arbitrary too — of interest, perhaps, only to those who happen to share the same values?

5 Social study and 'value freedom'

To explore this rather demoralizing argument further we must now consider its second step: is it true that the values of students of society necessarily affect their conclusions?

We may perhaps get a concrete sense of what is meant by this proposition by considering the all-too-frequent spectacle of professional economists, differing in their political views, developing radically different analyses of the current economic crisis on a television programme, during the course of which, if they are sensitive to the hopes of their producer, they get cross and shout at each other. Such disputants *seem* to be engaging in argument, certainly — but it doesn't seem to get them anywhere. How is this embarrassing phenomenon to be interpreted?

Those who take a view of morality similar to those we have been discussing will be tempted to point out that such fruitless debates bear all the marks of disputes about basic *moral* principles: they generate a good deal of heat, but at the end the disputants seem as far from each other as ever they were. And in fact, it may then be said, this hints at the true character of such economic debates. They are, in truth, conflicts of values. The economist from LSE is a left-winger, the financial correspondent of the *Daily Telegraph* politically Conservative. The apparent disagreement is protracted and irresolvable simply because it is in reality a collision between these two sets of moral and political beliefs: the economic theories of the two protagonists, it is thus being suggested, are reflections of their respective value judgements.

Somehow, then, economists' views about what is good in man and what would be good for society are supposed to feed into their process of investigation and theorizing, and so partly determine the conclusions they reach. And the same is true, it is said, throughout social science. There is no such thing as an 'objective' theory or research finding. Always they involve the relevant evaluations of their authors, and in consequence it is no surprise to find two social scientists with different 'evaluations' — with different moral or political outlooks — arguing indefinitely and fruitlessly over mutually incompatible conclusions.

6 *Possible mechanisms*

But at exactly what point is this 'feeding' process supposed to take place? What is the precise mechanism by which evaluations are introduced into a social investigation?

It is easy to think of ways in which they *might* be introduced. The student might select his facts in a biased way: an educationist who thought highly of the comprehensive ideal might derive results supporting his view by restricting his inquiry to relatively good comprehensive schools. Or the 'facts' themselves may be distorted by formulating a questionnaire so as to elicit wanted answers. These are but two of very many ways in which an inquirer's conclusions may be biased by his values — if the inquirer is not extremely careful.

But isn't care enough? Surely in cases such as these we may eliminate bias by giving close attention to our methodology. They illustrate traps for the unwary, which the wary may escape.

But the channels through which values feed into social study are not all of this kind, it is argued. Some *cannot* be blocked, so that the inquirer's conclusions are *necessarily* impregnated with his values, and not just accidentally, as a result of incompetent techniques.

One of the most searching arguments that have been put forward in defence of this thesis claims that the basic data of any social study cannot be *identified* without the involvement of value judgements: 'social facts', it is argued, can be picked out only with the use of concepts that are evaluative.

Steven Lukes develops a clear illustration in his concise and penetrating study, 'Relativism: Cognitive and Moral'. A common understanding of the notion of *power*, he tells us, among contemporary political scientists, is given by the proposition: one man exercises power over another when he affects the other in a manner contrary to the other's interests. But the notion of an *interest*, Lukes goes on, is irreducibly evaluative. What one takes to be a man's interest will be intimately bound up with one's moral and political views. A liberal, for example, will believe that a man's interests are to be identified with what that man actually thinks and says he wants, so that if I believe I want a newer car and fitted carpets my interest does indeed lie in my acquiring these things. But the radical political thinker, on the other hand, will hold that I myself may be deceived about my true interests. We succumb to the propaganda of capitalism when we think that what we want is a steadily rising material standard of living. Our *true* interest lies elsewhere — in the building of a humane, cooperative community.

Is governmental activity that encourages rising production in the motor car industry therefore an exercise of *power* or not? On the definition given, it is such only if it militates against people's interests. On the 'liberal' conception of interest, since people say they want new cars every few years, it cannot be an exercise of power (at least in this respect): but on the radical conception, such a government policy, by sustaining the status quo, would be working against people's true interests and so *would* be an exercise of power.

Apparently factual questions concerning power are thus shown to involve evaluations; and it is generally true, it has been suggested (Lukes does not in the paper claim this explicitly), that no social fact can be identified without the use of a concept that is 'value-laden' in the same sense.

I have tried to suggest that it is the thinker who believes that rational adjudication between rival basic moral beliefs is impossible, who will see one's whole understanding of social study as hanging on the thesis being defended by such arguments. If values do of necessity enter into the results of any social inquiry, then from this viewpoint there is something very embarrassingly 'non-objective' about them: whether people should in reason accept them will depend on whether they happen to share the values with which the results are informed. If they don't, nothing in reason can be said.

The best that can be done, it has been urged by at least some of those who accept the argument to this point, is for social inquirers to make clear, whenever they have a conclusion to report, just what the values were which informed the inquiry.

As perhaps is obvious, however, the argument is not completely irresistible. It is not clear, for one thing, that values do indeed inevitably feed into the social inquirer's conclusions. *Is* it true that social facts cannot be identified without the use of evaluative concepts? What is evaluative about the Census report, for example, that Cardiff has a population of about 275,000? And is it true, to take up the particular illustration worked out by Lukes — and accepting for the sake of argument the definition of 'power' that he discusses — that one's view of what lies in a person's interest depends on one's moral and political views? Might it not be the other way round — that the moral and political beliefs one arrives at will depend on one's views about what is in a person's interest, and that this is itself a view about a *factual* question? It is true that there is persistent disagreement about what is in a person's best interests, but is this fact enough to show that the issue is an 'evaluative' one? There has been persistent disagreement about the origin of the universe, but this points to the difficulty of establishing the facts, not to the non-factual, 'evaluative' character of the issue. To these points we shall return. Nor is it clear, moreover, that basic moral judgements are 'arbitrary'. Can it be true, one may indeed ask, incredulously, that one's basic moral beliefs are subject to neither rhyme nor reason? That there is nothing to be said against slavery, just so long as it is practised and approved within a different 'moral tradition' from one's own? Can one not rather speak of *right* and *mistaken* moral beliefs, of *better* or *worse* moral codes?

We begin to see how such ways of talking may indeed be defended —

may indeed reflect a sound conception of morality — when we pursue a question which 'non-objectivist' writers sometimes try to discredit: what is morality's *point*? Why is it there? What job does it do?

7 *Naturalist ethics*

These are questions that make very good sense to those thinkers we have discussed already who approach the human being as in his origins an *animal*.

One interesting account begins by pointing out that within the context of evolution the control of behaviour by reflective *consciousness* — that most mysterious phenomenon we stared at in an earlier chapter — is a relatively very recent development. Before that, natural selection had secured that the behaviour of an animal was adapted to the environment in which it found itself. This adaptation however, it is argued, would have taken two forms. On the one hand the animal would have developed ways of behaving which promoted its own individual survival. But on the other there would also have evolved patterns of behaviour that helped towards the survival not of the individual but of the *group* to which the individual belonged. The giving of warning signals would be an example here: the individual that gives one makes itself *individually* more vulnerable to attack, but the *group* is helped to escape.

With the evolution of man, however, the control of at least parts of the individual's behaviour is taken over by what we have just called the 'reflective consciousness': the organism begins to be able to choose what 'its' behaviour shall be, in the light of consciously considered reasons.

Whatever the adaptive advantages of this development, however, it has one vital demerit: it poses a threat to any patterns of behaviour engaged in by the individual which put the group's survival above the individual's own. For now they are conscious creatures they can raise the question: why should I ever consider the interests of the group? As one of the proponents of this view, the anthropologist Bernard Campbell, puts it: 'Man could see, as a result of his self-consciousness, how many of his activities were directed to satisfy his needs, his basic requirements for life; but he could also see that certain of his actions satisfied only social needs, that they led not to personal satisfaction but to frustration.'

There arises, therefore, the need for 'some device for directing a choice between possible actions', a need which is met *by a system of ethical beliefs*. 'Morality' thus arises, it is argued, as nature's way of ensuring that the group's survival is protected, even though this calls for self-sacrificial behaviour on the part of the individual.

On this conception, the *moral* is identified with *that which makes for group survival*, and reflection may well suggest great difficulties with it. There are other theories, however, of the same kind, some of which may seem less vulnerable. For example, the philosopher G. J. Warnock has recently defended in a careful and developed way the contention that the point of morality is 'the betterment ... of the human predicament', and this thesis shares with the evolutionary approach we have just been considering the vital feature of construing fundamental moral judgements as *not* arbitrary.

A principle that failed to contribute to group survival could not, on the evolutionary view, count as a moral principle at all; likewise, on Warnock's account, we can compare moral principles and judge which of them is better in the sense of helping more to alleviate man's lot. Where morality is thought of as having a *point*, of being there in order to fulfil some *function*, one might almost say, we can assess rival moral principles and alternative moral codes 'objectively'. We can judge between them according to the extent to which they help with what morality is there to do. The question of which principles are to be adopted becomes a factual matter, and the exclusive distinction between fact and value breaks down. Value judgements become a sort of factual judgement.

Such a 'naturalist' conception of morality has the effect of diminishing in importance the arguments over whether social study can be 'value-free'. If matters of value are matters of fact, what is important is not so much that inquirers' values should not enter into their conclusions, but that their values should be *correct*.

Here, then, we have one response to the arguments which purport to show that the student of society cannot avoid encapsulating his values in his conclusions. The claim is ceded; but, by setting it alongside an *objectivist* conception of morality, it is argued that social study can none the less be free of arbitrariness.

12 Social study and bias

1 *Difficulty of social study*

We have seen that one response to the arguments purporting to show that social inquirers' values necessarily feed into their conclusions is to suggest that, since matters of value are also matters of fact, the arguments don't much matter: even if valid they do *not* show that such conclusions are infected with arbitrariness.

Another, as I have indicated, is to urge that the arguments are in fact to be rejected. It is just not true, according to this line of thought, that social inquirers' values inevitably figure in their conclusions.

For those who take this view, however, there is still to be accounted for the lack of agreement among social students, the seemingly irresolvable conflicts which our economic debate was meant to exemplify. If social study *can* be objective, why do we find even leading figures in social 'science' speaking with very different voices on the same issue?

It is argued that, leaving the matter of evaluation aside altogether, there is intrinsically more scope for disagreement in social study than there is in natural science, because support for any particular proposition or theory is so much harder to build.

1.1 *Controlled experimentation.* Within natural science it is usually possible to use rigorous investigative techniques in which the objects under study are brought into the laboratory. There they may be subject to precisely known environmental conditions, which may be

varied, within limits, in known ways, and their responses continuously monitored. For example, a biologist wishing to discover the effect of a certain chemical substance on the growth of a given type of plant can take genetically identical specimens into his laboratory. Then, feeding half of them with the substance and leaving the rest untreated (they act as the 'control'), he can compare reactions; and because he may reasonably assume that all the other conditions are the same for both groups, he can conclude that any differences between the two growth patterns are due to the chemical under test.

The use of even this rigorous type of controlled experimentation does not yield the certainty that perhaps one might be tempted to ascribe to it at first, for no worker can be certain that *all* the conditions (save the factor under test) are identical for the compared groups; and other forms of close laboratory observation and experiments are perhaps not quite so rigorous as the controlled experiment in its strictest form. Nevertheless, the sort of evidence that can be produced by this kind of work can plausibly be said to have considerable strength. It is evidence of this kind, however (so it is alleged), that is usually not obtainable as far as social study is concerned.

Consider the hypothesis that capital punishment deters potential murderers, for example. We may think quickly that a way of testing this would be to look at the murder rates in all countries that practised capital punishment and compare them with the murder rates for countries that had abolished it. But a test like this would be inadequate because every country differs in very many respects from any other country, and the differential murder rates could be due to differences in factors quite independent of the existence of the death penalty.

If we could introduce two countries into the controlled environment of the laboratory and arrange, so far as we could, that each enjoyed exactly the same conditions as the other, and then abolish the death penalty in just the one ... we should have a situation that would clearly yield powerful evidence one way or another on the question at issue; but even more clearly, if only on the crudest considerations of scale, it would be impossible to set up. Instead, we have to make up our minds on this important question by considering evidence of a very much more problematic kind. Looking at the relatively high murder figures for Mortalia, where they don't have the death penalty, leads me, let us say, to the view that the capital sanction is indeed a deterrent. But you point out that there are many differences between Mortalia and Britain besides the one involving the death penalty, and the difference in murder rate is in your view due rather to one of these: the result, perhaps, of the lower standard of living. For your part you urge me to look at the figures for Arcadia, where they have no death penalty and a low murder rate — showing, as you claim, that the death penalty has nothing to do with keeping murder rates low. But the fact that the murder rate in Arcadia is low by British standards, I point out, does not mean that it would not be lower if the death penalty were introduced.

With comparative figures for a wide variety of different countries, and with figures for countries that have experimented with abolishing the death penalty, and particularly with the statistical techniques that may be applied to derive what is significant from all these figures, the evidence for and against the deterrent effect of capital punishment can be a good deal more substantial than the informal argument I have sketched suggests. But it remains true, surely, that the impossibility of controlled experimentation significantly increases the difficulty with which such a claim may be substantiated.

1.2 *Ethical constraints.*   As I pointed out, the sheer scale of the enterprise of bringing whole countries into a 'laboratory' is perhaps the most striking impossibility in applying the method of controlled experimentation to the problem we have been discussing. But another obstacle, which stands in the way of other kinds of rigorous investigative procedures too, is presented by considerations of *morality* itself. It would be extremely helpful in the study of the development of the human infant, for example, to isolate a series of actual 'specimens' in the laboratory where they could be subject to a precisely known environment and continuous monitoring. (The particular question, much debated in some quarters, of the extent to which the development of language would take place in the absence of all contact with other human beings could be answered by the simplest of isolation experiments.) But most people (at least) would agree that such procedures would be out of the question for *ethical* reasons. No one has the right to interfere with a developing human being in the way that they demand.

These are just two of a number of reasons for expecting social study to be exceedingly difficult. By comparison with the natural sciences, it is much more problematic to support one's claims or theories with really compelling evidence.

From this fact, it is then said, a very significant consequence follows: on any one issue a variety of incompatible theses are likely to develop, no one of which can be shown to be indefensible. The rigorous methods of selection between rival theories which are available in natural science are not applicable, and, whatever view a particular thinker adopts, he will be able to offer a more or less reasonable defence of it. It is thus concluded that, even if the conclusions of social inquiry are purely factual in character (either because such conclusions can be free of values or because, though they are involved, matters of value are themselves factual), there is good reason to expect difficulty in establishing them, and good reason to expect different people to espouse rival theories, none of which can be shown to be substantially superior to the others.

2 *Ideology*

It may be argued that, even where natural science is concerned, factors that have nothing to do with the evidence for a particular theory influence people's response to it; but the role of such factors in influencing the acceptance of claims arising out of *social* study can be seen to be even greater; for in the social sphere, I have just been arguing, the evidence for any particular conclusion is even less conclusive. The question of what such logically 'irrelevant' factors might be is of correspondingly greater importance.

The approach to this question, which I wish to explain because of its importance and influence (far beyond the confines of academic social study), begins by noticing that some beliefs seem to be tied up with the structure of a society as it is at any particular time.

2.1 *The ethics of 'usury'*. Take, for example, the question of whether money should be lent on the promise of *interest*.

This is a practice upon which the organization of our society, as it is at present, depends. The capital to finance industrial activity is put together by persuading people to lend sums of money on the understanding that if all goes well they will get back more than they put up. Clearly this mechanism would be considerably hampered, to say the least, if there was a widespread and deeply felt conviction that making money simply by lending it in this way was morally wrong.

It is very interesting to realize, therefore, that in the feudal world out of which capitalism arose such a moral judgement *was* generally made. 'Money is barren,' Aristotle had said, and it was generally agreed when the feudal system was at its height that it could not be right for someone to make a profit or, even more plainly, a living, by doing absolutely nothing save lend out his money. It could not be right for money by itself to *make* money. The term 'usury' expresses even today something of the medievals' condemnation of the practice: they thought it rather squalid.

Gradually, however, the idea of money being lent out and a return expected became less and less objectionable to people as industrial society developed, until it has become, in the end, to seem to many entirely reasonable. What used to be regarded as morally disgraceful comes to be accepted as unexceptionable. And we are led to think, therefore, that men's moral judgement is indeed linked somehow with the way in which their society is organized. Moral condemnation of usury flourishes when it does no economic harm, but by some mechanism comes to decline when economic developments would be hindered by its persistence.

2.2 *The rationality of 'unlimited desires'.*　Perhaps more controversially, it has also been argued that people's attitude to the accumulation of wealth underwent a related change during the same economic transition.

The mechanism of industrialization by capitalism relied, it is argued, on prospective investors wanting to grow rich — it was this prospect that persuaded them to lend their money and so create the necessary capital. But when the initial lending and return had been made, it was vital that the lender should be prepared to lend again: otherwise capital for continued expansion would not be available. It was necessary, therefore, not only for prospective investors to want more money, and so be prepared to invest, but for them to go on wanting more and more money indefinitely, so that when a return had been made they would go on investing with the hope of even greater return. A person with this kind of insatiable desire to go on accumulating wealth might well strike us even today when we stand back a little as simply greedy. We can surely understand the feeling that it can only be a kind of moral delinquency that could lead a man to want to grow richer and richer and richer without end.

It was just such a feeling, it is claimed, that was widespread and deeply felt in pre-capitalist society. People were acknowledged to have a right to satisfy their ordinary human needs — for food and drink, clothing and shelter — but not to go on accumulating wealth indefinitely. The desire to do so would have been seen as a miser's irrationality, a piece of moral pathology.

Yet, with the emergence of the new economic order, this severely critical attitude is replaced by one that condones unlimited accumulation. It becomes accepted that man's desires are unlimited, and that no matter what a man has, no matter how rich he is, it is entirely reasonable for him to want more. People come to recognize, in the jargon of political philosophy, 'a right to infinite accumulation'. Once again we have it suggested, therefore, that beliefs — in this case moral beliefs — are linked to the structure of society. More particularly we have the suggestion that a given society will be characterized by those general beliefs that support its essential activities: and beliefs that tend to undermine those activities will not be widespread.

2.3 *Possible mechanisms.* Those who take this view have the obligation to explain what the crucial mechanism is, of course: how exactly does it come about that only what one might call 'functional' beliefs become widespread?

We shall return to this problem later, in relation to 'functionalism' in general. Here we notice the very influential answer that is given by Left-leaning political thought.

Most societies with which we are familiar, it is claimed, are divided into *classes* which differ in the amount of privilege they enjoy: people live in luxury or in poverty or perhaps somewhere between the two depending on the class to which they belong. Those that live well will have an interest in conserving the society in its existing form, for it gives them their relative privilege; and the suggestion arises very naturally that these privileged members of any society will generally do all they can to maintain the status quo — including the fostering, among the people at large, of such beliefs as will help with that objective.

Karl Marx, in developing the most influential version of this line of thought, seems almost to speak of the privileged class as literally hiring people with the requisite talents to put about such 'conservative' beliefs: intellectuals, artists, priests and philosophers regarded as being actually commissioned to develop and promulgate such ideas and images as may be calculated to support the existing order. Members of the ruling class would then have to be endowed with a total cynicism: knowing certain beliefs to be false, they would nevertheless be putting them about for 'reasons of security', as I suppose it could be put.

Another mechanism by which 'conservative' notions might become inculcated in people at large would involve the general psychological thesis that given the chance people will believe what they *want* to believe. According to this principle, a person (for example) who has devoted his life to campaigning against racial discrimination is likely to want to believe that there are no racially correlated differences in intelligence and therefore to reject experimental work leading to that conclusion, unless the evidence in support of it is really compelling. Similarly, perhaps one might suggest that a man who enjoys fishing is likely to want to believe that a hooked fish feels no pain; and accordingly to adopt this belief in the absence of really telling contrary evidence.

Applied to members of the privileged class, the principle means that they will tend to adopt beliefs which in one way or another would help to justify the social structure which supports them in privilege, because these are the beliefs they will want to have. A successful businessman in a capitalist economy such as our own who has built his success on an unswerving practice of ruthlessly hard, unscrupulous dealing will want to believe, it seems plausible to suggest, that people are generally selfish, so that if he hadn't trampled on others, they would have trampled on him; and since it is as difficult to oppose such a conception of man with compelling evidence as it is to support it, he will, because he wants to, maintain it.

If this thinking is right, it is exactly 'conservative' beliefs that we should expect the privileged themselves to entertain. The concluding step is then simple: since the privileged class in any society will at least (according to the political Left) also be the most influential, it will be *their* view of the world that is purveyed through every important organ of communication. That view will be purveyed, however, not because its conservative effect has been *calculated*, but because, as I have just explained, those in power have persuaded themselves that it is *correct*.

2.4 *Bias in social study.*   We have been looking at two general claims, then, about beliefs that are widespread in society. The first is that such beliefs tend to be those that support the established order, and the second is that the mechanism by which such beliefs become widespread springs from our propensity — given the opportunity — to believe what we want.

How do these claims appear when they are applied to the particular case of social study? Is it true that the conventionally accepted ideas in *this* field are accepted not because of the merits of whatever case supports them but because *they* support the established order?

Critics of conventional social study in the West have argued in the affirmative by pointing to the very framework within which that study is conducted. The very idea, they say, of there being *more than one* social science — that economics, sociology, political science and psychology are separable disciplines — enshrines at the most basic level a conservative world-view.

Thus, a Marxist opponent of capitalist society would claim that what human beings think and do, and what social organization they partake in, can be understood only in the light of the need to meet their necessities of life — food, clothing, shelter — and of the ways of fulfilling this need that are open to them. The *economic* organization of a society — the way in which it meets this need — thus informs (although it doesn't necessarily determine) the other aspects of the life of its members. To separate the study of sociology, therefore, from the study of economics (just to take one example), as is done institutionally in British and American universities and in the publication of associated research work, etc., is to distract attention away from the possibility of the economic facts throwing light on sociological questions, and away from the thesis that major problems within capitalist society will only be resolved by a revolution in its economic basis.

If we go on to ask by what mechanism the beliefs of social students might be thus influenced in a conservative direction we can see that the general mechanism sketched above might be invoked. It has been true, at any rate, that professional academics in the social studies area enjoy a relatively privileged position within Western society, so that their interest will lie in preserving the status quo. But there is also the fact, it might be said, that the finance for their academic activities is provided from establishment sources; besides which it may be noted that the way into the profession is open only to those who are prepared to work within the established framework for, say, half a dozen years (three as an undergraduate, and as many again as a supervised postgraduate student). None of this amounts to the claim that students of society have their beliefs within their field of study imposed upon them by their situation. The suggestion that emerges from this line of argument is rather that, despite the possibility of objective work, it will take an exceptionally strong mind to resist the power of the several biasing influences upon it.

13 Society and its members

1 *Reductionism*

In social study, we have been saying, the conception of the human being with which we start out will influence our approach. But the same is true of our conception of society, and this is the matter we turn to now.

Perhaps the most basic question, and one that in a sense underlies all the others that I have space to raise, is *whether societies exist in their own right at all.* For surely, it may be argued, a society is simply a collection of individual human beings, so that the existence of a society is no more and no less than the existence of those human beings; and, more pertinently, once we agree that a society is no more and no less than the individuals who belong to it, mustn't we agree that in understanding how the individual behaves we shall be understanding all there is to understand about society? On this showing sociology, for example, becomes something of a bogus enterprise. It is the concern of psychology to find out about the individual, it may be said, and if a society is made up entirely of individuals there will surely be nothing else to find out about?

This 'reductionist' view of social reality and correspondingly of social study receives its classical formulation in some words of J. S. Mill:

> ... the laws of the phenomena of society are, and can be, nothing but the laws of the actions and passions of human beings united together in the social state. Men, however, in a state of society,

are still men: their actions and passions are obedient to the laws
of individual human nature ... Human beings in society have no
properties but those which are derived from, and may be resolved
into, the laws of the nature of individual man.

Mill thus accepts the point that a society is made up exclusively of
the individuals who belong to it and, applying the reductionist
principle, arrives at the conclusion that all social phenomena are to
be wholly explained 'in terms of facts about individuals'. A jargon
term that is often applied to this position — and to relatives of it —
is 'methodological individualism'.

2 *Its significance*

At first sight the view as outlined here may seem straightforward
enough: but reflection (true to irritating form) soon dissolves the
straightforwardness away. The fundamental difficulty lies in clarify-
ing what *counts* as 'a fact about the individual', and following on
from that in reaching a clear understanding of what exactly is being
denied by the 'methodological individualist's' claims that facts
about society boil down to facts about individuals, and that therefore sociology is 'reducible' to psychology.

Suppose it were true, for example, that whenever 'the individual
man' joined an excited crowd his powers of criticism dwindled, he
immediately picked up and adopted the feelings of those around
him, his inhibitions dropped away, and so on, and so on. Suppose,
that is to say, we had established a law of how the human being
reacted when part of a crowd. The question is, to put it in Mill's
terms: would this be a 'law of the nature of individual man'?

Or take the case of an inquiry into why people vote in the way they
do. The finding may be that people are influenced by their standard
of living, by where they live, and by the sort of people their parents
were. Is a finding like this a truth about 'the individual man'? It
seems harmless to accept this way of putting it — so long as it is
acknowledged that voting is a *social* act, and can only take place
within a group context.

But if methodological individualism is to be construed as allowing
facts like these as facts about the individual, what exactly is it to be
understood as denying? What is there in the approaches and
practices of sociology (for example) that methodological individualism would condemn? Some thinkers have thought: nothing much.
Methodological individualism is a doctrine that to begin with sounds
bold and iconoclastic, but which in the end proves difficult to

interpret meaningfully at all; and the considerable debate over whether to accept it has all been in consequence rather a waste of time.

Yet in that debate, it has seemed to others (and to me), there are buried important questions about the nature of society.

3 *Society as an individual*

One meaningful and important point that 'methodological individualists', or those shall we say who take a 'reductionist' view, may be making is that a society is not analogous to an *individual*, in the sense in which a person is an individual. Consider, for example, Isaiah Berlin's account of the approach to understanding societies of the influential nineteenth-century philosopher G. W. F. Hegel: 'Hegel transferred the concept of the personal character of the individual, the aims, logic, quality of his thoughts, his choices — his whole activity as it unfolds itself throughout a man's life — to the case of entire cultures and nations.' Part of the immense importance of Hegel, Berlin goes on to tell us, lies 'in the field of social and historical studies, in the creation of new disciplines, which consist in the history and criticism of human institutions, viewed as great collective quasi-personalities, which possess a life and character of their own, and cannot be described purely in terms of the individuals who compose them', and leading, Berlin concludes, to 'the treatment of state, race, history, epoch, for example, as super-persons exercising influence' which constitute irrational and dangerous myths.

To try to clarify what it is to treat a society as a 'super-person' we must raise the difficult and abstract question of what it is to *be* an 'individual'. An inkling of what is involved may be obtained by considering the assembly of an amplifier, for example. In a context such as this one can see the sense in the idea that before assembly the separate parts exist 'in their own right', whereas once incorporated into the new structure they lose their 'independent existence' and become part of something else. Before, they were individuals, 'things in their own right'; after, there is just *one* individual, the newly assembled amplifier, of which they have become the parts.

Another suggestive contrast is the one between a population of unicellular organisms and a simple multicellular organism. The multicellular organism consists entirely of single cells; yet again one can understand the sense in saying that in the population of unicells there are many individuals existing independently in their own right, while in the multicellular organism there is a single individual made up of many components.

It is instructive to think of the fascinating slime-moulds in this connection, too, for this is a form of organic life that alternates between uni- and multi-cellularity. Sometimes slime-mould is represented by single cells that live independently of each other; but under certain conditions a number of individual cells move towards each other and link up to form a new composite structure, which proceeds to move about and otherwise behave like a single multi-cellular organism. When this happens, many individuals merge their identities, one might say, to yield the single identity of the new structure. *Many* individuals become *one*. Subsequently, when conditions change again, the single body disintegrates and the independent life of what were its components is re-established: *one* individual becomes *many*.

We can begin to see sense in the claim that a society is a 'super-person' by construing it as the claim that a society is an 'individual' in the sense I am trying to arrive at here. Going beyond the merely suggestive considerations I have been putting forward to say exactly what is meant by claiming that a society is an individual (and not a mere collection of individuals) and what precisely is the point and importance of such a claim is not easy. But one matter arises clearly out of the passage from Berlin.

If we treat the state as an individual, he suggests, then our *political* considerations may well be different from what they would otherwise be. For when we try to work out what sort of social arrangements will be most favourable to everybody's interests it will then not be enough to consider the interests of all the *citizens* of the state: we shall also have to consider the interests of the state itself. And, indeed, the tendency of those who have apparently sympathized with Hegel on this point has not been to minimize the importance of the state's interests. Under men like Mussolini, for example, often alleged to be deeply influenced by Hegelian thought, it is the individual citizen's significance that pales in comparison with what is alleged to be the state's.

This little that I have said about a society's or a state's being an 'individual' doesn't take us very far. But it enables us to go on to make an important distinction which is blurred in the passage I quoted from Berlin.

In that passage, Hegel is convicted of treating groups of persons as themselves 'super-persons' — groups of individuals as themselves individuals, as I have put it. But Berlin goes straight on to say, almost as though it follows logically, that Hegel holds of these 'super-persons' that they 'cannot be described purely in terms of the individuals who compose them'. It may be important to stress, however, that the second of these claims does *not* follow from the first —

at least if the latter is construed on anything like the lines I have suggested.

Think of reductionism in the field of biology. The reductionist does not wish to deny that, for example, the many individual cells of the slime-mould, when they come together to form the single composite body, form a new single individual. All they say is that such an individual's properties must be explicable in terms of the properties of the component parts. Similarly, the reductionist view of relatively ordinary multicellular organisms like worms or birds is not that they do not comprise individual organisms but that they can be understood in terms of the properties of the cells that compose them.

In biology, then, the assertion that an animal (say) is an individual is quite distinct from the assertion that its properties can never be fully explained in terms of the properties of its parts. Reductionists in this field do not contest the former claim — all agree that organisms are individuals. It is the latter that they reject.

When we come back to the question of reductionist conceptions of society, however, we encounter the fact that there is no corresponding general agreement that a society is an 'individual' and so the possibility of a form of reductionism to which there is in biological thought no analogue. One interesting if enigmatic claim that methodological individualists may be making, then — to put it the other way round — is that societies are not individuals in the sense alluded to.

4 *Durkheim on the reality of society*

A second possibility develops the second idea presented by Berlin: that societies 'cannot be described purely in terms of the individuals who compose them'. The character of this type of reductionism emerges most clearly, perhaps, if we set it against the approach to social study it thinks illegitimate. That of the great sociological pioneer Émile Durkheim will serve as representative.

As a matter of fact Durkheim's thought is 'anti-reductionist' in the first sense we distinguished, too; for he believed that a society is to be regarded as an individual. 'Society', he says, 'is not a mere sum of individuals. Rather the system formed by their association represents a specific reality which has its own characteristics.' But he went beyond this to claim that these characteristics could not be explained in terms of the characteristics of society's 'components' — its members.

Durkheim's idea is that when individuals come together in the form of a society, phenomena 'emerge' which are on a different level from those in which the individual considered as an individual could be involved. To pick up the example we used above: no individual who did not belong to a society could ever be described as 'casting a vote'; but where individuals have come together to form a society, the 'phenomenon' of voting may emerge. In a similar but by no means identical way, a society of individuals may be said to have, for example, a complicated legal code, whereas such a thing could never be said of an individual. Durkheim himself draws attention to the parallel that does arise in this case with biological thought. Organisms, he argues, display all the distinctive phenomena of life — for example, they assimilate food and reproduce — in spite of the fact that the inorganic atoms of which they are ultimately made up individually display none of these phenomena. They must be considered, therefore, to 'arise' or 'emerge' when (asserts (Durkheim) the atoms come together. It is clear in the biological case, says Durkheim, that what is distinctive about living things must be a consequence not of the properties of their components but of the way they are *organized* (Durkheim's term is perhaps best translated as 'associated'). It is the same with a society. Distinctively social phenomena are a consequence not (only) of the properties of individual men but of the way those individuals are organized vis-à-vis each other. Thus the passage we have already quoted has an explanatory sequel:

> Society is not a mere sum of individuals. Rather, the system formed by their association represents a specific reality which has its own characteristics. Of course, nothing collective can be produced if individual consciousnesses are not assumed; but this necessary condition is by itself insufficient. These consciousnesses must be combined in a certain way; social life results from this combination and is, consequently, explained by it.

5 *A parallel in biological thought*

To become clearer about Durkheim's position on this point it is, I think, helpful to pursue his allusion to biology, for there we find a doctrine — known as 'organismic biology' — which closely parallels his own position with regard to sociology.

'Organisms', writes Paul Weiss, expounding the 'organismic' concept, 'are not just heaps of molecules'. It may be true that they are made up of *nothing but* molecules; yet the molecules are *organized* in a particular way, and it is this fact that the reductionist principle ignores. For some of the properties of the organism as a whole are a consequence, according to the organismic biologist, not of the properties of the parts but of the organization by which those parts are unified. Thus it is that a motor car has different properties from those of the heap of scrap iron that would result if it were simply taken to pieces: properties produced by the organization of the various parts in a very particular way.

Biology, they conclude, will therefore never reduce to physics, for an understanding of organisms will never follow solely from an understanding of the physical parts of which, it is conceded, they are indeed composed. It is only when a knowledge of the parts is supplemented by a knowledge of the organization uniting them that an understanding of the complex whole becomes possible.

Against the organismic biologist, however, it might be argued that he has not pushed his line of thought far enough. It may be true that the organization of a set of parts influences the properties of the whole; but, it may be argued, that organization is itself merely the consequence of the properties of the component parts.

Consider, for example, what happens when a concentrated solution of (common) salt is left exposed in a pan. The water gradually evaporates and crystals of salt are formed. These crystals are three-dimensional solid structures consisting of sodium and chlorine ions related to each other in a precisely ordered way, and it is upon this structure that some of the properties of the crystal depend. But what determines the structure, it is argued, is the nature of the components: it is the structure of the chlorine component and the structure of the sodium component which determine the structure, and thus the properties, of the crystal they form together. Once again we should conclude that a knowledge of the parts suffices for an understanding of the whole, and the reductionist principle stands.

This defence of the principle serves, however, to reveal its limitations, for it seems clear that not all complex wholes are like crystals of salt. A protein molecule, for example, is composed of molecules of amino acid, but, unlike the sodium and chlorine ions in the salt, the amino acid molecules are able to link up with each other in a huge variety of different ways. If we take a protein molecule and ask what determined the organization of its parts, we cannot in this case answer 'their structure'; for the structures of the parts are compatible with many different structures of the whole. The answer instead is that their manner of linking up is dictated by the structure of another molecule — ultimately, as the theory of protein synthesis tells us, the structure of a molecule of DNA. In this case, therefore, what determines the organization of the (protein) molecule is not one or more of its parts but something that is not one of its parts at all, something that is *external*.

A much more familiar example is provided by the organization shown by the bricks of a house. That organization is not a consequence simply of the nature of the bricks. Rather it is imposed on the bricks by 'something' which is not a part of the house at all — by the man who built it.

There are cases, it is thus argued, where the reductionist principle does not apply. When the structure of a complex entity is determined from outside (when it is 'externally directed', as it might be put), an understanding of the properties of the parts will *not* yield an understanding of the properties of the whole. It will be necessary also for the latter to acquire an understanding of the agency responsible for the parts' organization.

Perhaps Durkheim's 'anti-reductionist' views of society may be understood in this light. He says that distinctively social phenomena are a consequence of the organization of the individuals belonging to a society. But the reductionist might try to argue that such organization must itself be a consequence of the 'properties' of the individuals who belong to it. What gives rise to social organization — the relationships people have to each other in society — he may ask, if it is not the psychology of the individual? Durkheim's reply is that the individual is always born into a social organization, from which he learns his distinctively social behaviour. The social organization of one generation, as it were, is thus the basic determinant of the next. I interpret this as a version of the idea I have just presented — that the organization of individuals in a society is 'externally directed': it springs not solely from the 'properties' of the individuals concerned, but is strongly influenced too by the existing structure of the society into which the individual is born.

We have, therefore, a second conception of society which a reductionist may wish to reject, a second intepretation, in other words, of 'methodological individualism', denying not that a society is in some sense an 'individual' but denying that it possesses properties which cannot be explained by the properties of its members.

According to this latter sort of reductionism, as we noted earlier, 'sociology' is not a discipline in its own right; there is no study of individuals grouped to form a society to be distinguished from the study of the individuals themselves. It was this implication that Durkheim was most concerned to invalidate. Writing not so much an apologia for a going concern as a manifesto for an enterprise yet to be developed, Durkheim was concerned to show that sociology was to be a science with a subject matter quite distinctly of its own. It was to consist of the study of *social* phenomena, in its attempt to understand the development and function of the *social* 'institutions' (religion, ethics, law, for example) such phenomena represent.

The autonomy of sociology is thus one great issue which reductionism in this area bears upon. But it is also bound up with another important issue — which we now discuss in its own right — raised by Durkheim when he says that part of the sociologist's task is to show the 'function' of whatever social fact we are concerned with 'in the establishment of social order'. It is the question of the implications and legitimacy of the approach to social study known as 'functionalism'.

14 Society as a working system

1 *Introduction*

The reaction of a rabbit to approaching danger is to beat the ground with its rear feet before making for cover. Biologists interpret such behaviour as constituting a *warning signal*: it is supposed to warn the rest of the rabbit group of the danger that one of them has recognized. The biologist here is asking of something that an animal does what its *point* is, and he is providing an answer in terms of the contribution it makes to the survival of the group. To the question — what is the function of the rabbit's stamping the ground like that? — he supplies the answer: 'it serves to warn others of approaching danger, and thus improves the chances of the group's escaping unharmed.'

Sustained attempts have been made to apply the same type of analysis to certain kinds of human behaviour. It is appropriate to inquire, it has been suggested, into the *point* of some of the things human beings do, and to look for an answer in terms of the contribution the particular activity makes to the survival of the group concerned. Religious practices, for example, have been said to serve the function of binding the individuals in a society closely together so that a unified group is maintained.

The great anthropologist Bronislaw Malinowski developed an extreme formulation of this approach. He held that we can expect *every* element or 'component' of a society to perform a necessary function, and thus puts forward an extreme version of the doctrine best called *classical societal functionalism*: 'The functional view ...

insists ... upon the principle that in every type of civilization, every custom, material object, idea and belief fulfils some vital function, has some task to accomplish, represents an indispensable part within a working whole.'

With the reference to a 'working whole' the analogy proposed here between a society and a *machine* is virtually explicit. The functionalist, as this passage refers to him, invites us to think of a society as though it were a machine, and on that basis to conceive of the sociologist's task as that of determining the function of each of its components. For any machine to work, certain interdependent interlocking functions have to be performed. In a petrol engine, for example, something has to inject the fuel, something has to control the timing of the ignition, something else has to ensure the synchronization of the fuel intake and exhaust valves, and so on. If any of these essential functions were not performed, the engine would not work. In the same way, according to classical societal functionalism, there are certain functions that must be performed by the components of a society. If they are not, then the society will not be able to 'work' either. It is reasonable to think that there must be, for example, a set of rules — acknowledged as valid by people generally — by appeal to which disputes between individuals may be settled; otherwise, with individuals simply fighting it out, no society would be possible at all.

For some decades now the classical form of functionalism we have just described has been virtually criticized to death. It stands accused of committing the 'sin' of 'teleology', as Marion Levy puts it, and I want now to try to make plain what this charge, clearly a thing of dreadful gravity, amounts to.

2 *Purpose*

The critic begins by pointing out that it doesn't make sense to apply 'functional analysis' to *everything*. The planet Jupiter, for example, forms part of the solar system; and yet the question of the *function* of Jupiter's orbiting the sun surely strikes us as inappropriate. Similarly, it is true that a salt crystal is made up of component atoms (or, better, 'radicals'): but it is surely not relevant to look for the function of any of them. On the other hand, we *can* legitimately speak, surely, of the function of the scarifier on a steamroller, or the function of the treasurer of a club.

If your 'intuitions' agree with mine over these examples, they tell us that 'functional analysis' applies to some things but not to others; and the question arises: what then is the difference between the two sorts of things?

The answer, so it seems very plausible to suggest, has something to do with *purposes* or *goals* or '*ends*'. The steamroller is constructed with some purpose in mind, and *this*, it might be suggested, gives us the justification for asking about the function of one of its parts; and similarly we can speak of the function of a club treasurer because the club presumably has some purpose behind it — the purpose for which it was set up. Outside a religious framework, on the other hand, there is no purpose behind the solar system, and no one puts together a crystal with some end in view: hence, it is proposed, the inappropriateness of functional analysis in instances such as these. According to this line of thought, what makes functional analysis appropriate is the fact that a thing has some purpose or goal.

The point can be supported from another direction. Think of the workings of a car engine and of the difference between saying that the sparking plugs *cause* the fuel and air mixture to ignite and saying that the ignition of the mixture is the *function* of the plugs. What more do we say in invoking the notion of 'function'? We say, surely, that not only do the plugs have a certain effect but also that, unless they did, and so long as nothing else took their place, the engine *would not work*. But with reference to the engine's *working* we are committed to the idea that it has some purpose or goal. These parts were put together so that the completed system *would* work, and each part is functional in so far as it contributes to the achievement of this goal. From a second starting point, therefore, we reach the contention that one cannot ask for the function of a part of a system unless there is an answer to the question: to the achievement of what purpose or goal does the part contribute?

Having made this point, the critic of classical societal functionalism applies it to the case of societies. He asks whether a *society* can be said to have a purpose or goal.

Some people seem to think that the answer to this question must be quite obviously No. They seem to assume that a purpose is necessarily something that is conceived in a mind, so that if a thing is to be said to have a purpose it must either itself possess a mind — that is, must be a 'conscious agent' — or it must have been *created* by a 'conscious agent'. But neither of these can be true of *societies*. Societies are *made up* of conscious agents — people — certainly, and these people are capable both of having purposes and of endowing their artefacts with purposes. The society to which they belong, however, is surely *not* itself a conscious agent, nor is it something that has been made by a conscious agent with some purpose in mind (unless one takes a bold religious view). The notion of its having a purpose or goal, it is thus concluded, must be inadmissible.

A quick way with classical functionalism is thus to say that it implies that the society to which it is applied is capable of conceiving of purposes, which is absurd.

3   *Goal-directed behaviour*

Some would argue, however, that this way is *too* quick, relying on too narrow an interpretation of 'having a purpose or goal'. The narrowness comes out immediately one recognizes that *biologists* feel no qualms about applying functional analysis to animals and plants. It is said, for example, that the function of the nemocyst cells in hydra is to inject prey with poison, and that the function of the stomata on plant leaves is to permit the circulation of gases. When we pose the significant question formulated above — what is the goal towards the achievement of which the part in question contributes? — we get the same reply in both cases: the goal is the survival of the organism concerned. Without nemocysts or nemocyst substitutes a hydra could not survive, just as a plant could not go on living if nothing did the job of the stomata.

It is sensible, on this account, to speak of non-human organisms, and even of organisms that must surely be pretty well non-conscious, as capable of having goals, so that the notion of having a goal is being construed as covering more than the straightforward case of someone *thinking* of a purpose which they then pursue in their actions.

What, then, is it to 'have a goal' in this wider sense? If it is not simply a matter of consciously entertained aims, what is it? What is the difference between a system that has a goal and one that does not?

One attempt to define the difference has been to say that a so-called 'goal-directed' system is one which shows in its behaviour 'persistence towards some end state, under varying conditions'. The plant on my window sill, for example, alters the orientation of its leaves whenever it is turned away from the sun. Its 'end state' in this respect could be said to be the exposure of the maximum surface area of leaf to the sunlight, and the 'varying conditions' are those I impose by partially rotating the plant. However I turn it, the leaves twist round to achieve once more their optimum orientation. The hunting bird of prey provides another example. Its 'goal' or 'end state' is the capture of some small animal, but it does not find its quarry in a fixed spot. It has to ignore varying physical conditions, searching for prey until successful.

This suggested definition also seems to fit certain artefacts. A thermostatically controlled heating system, for example, maintains the end state of a steady internal temperature in spite of fluctuating temperatures outside. A guided missile seeks its target despite evasive action that the latter might undertake. And it fits human purposive behaviour as well. A newspaper reporter, attempting to get an interview with a reluctant celebrity, may begin by phoning for an appointment. If that fails, he may try the direct approach of walking up to the house. Turned away at the lodge, he may scale the wall. Thrown out of the grounds, he may next seek access under the guise of delivering the groceries. Here the behaviour of the 'system' (the reporter), although known to be guided by a preconceived purpose, follows the pattern we have just noticed: there is 'persistence towards an end state' (the interview) in the face of 'varying conditions'.

There can be 'goal-directed' behaviour without conscious purpose: that is the gist of this view. We can pick it out from behaviour that is not goal-directed simply on the basis of what we observe. We see a bird of prey quartering the ground and we can tell that its behaviour is goal-directed just by looking; we don't have to ask ourselves whether the bird *has in mind* the securing of food. In observing the reorientation of leaves towards the light we can say that their behaviour is 'directed towards a goal' without the ridiculous implication that the plant is consciously aware of its needs and acts accordingly.

Although the validity of the category of 'goal-directed behaviour' is recognized by many thinkers, we notice that they are mostly agreed in rejecting the actual definition we have been suggesting. One weakness, for example, is that it would allow into the category the behaviour of a river flowing down hill, which is usually assumed to be an intuitively clear case of behaviour that is *not* really 'goal-directed'. Nevertheless, it is still possible to affirm the sense in *looking* for such a definition — to agree, in other words, that there is a category of 'goal-directed behaviour' which is wider than that of behaviour informed by preconceived purposes, and that 'functional analysis' can be applied to representatives of the wider class as well as to those of the narrower.

It may be conceded, therefore, that we can only speak of the *function* of a part of a thing when there is an answer to the question: what is the goal towards the achievement of which the part contributes? But the *goal* here need not be a preconceived purpose — it need not be an aim actually entertained by a mind.

As far as sociology is concerned, therefore, the question that arises is whether a society constitutes a goal-directed system in the wider sense. Granted the absurdity of the idea of its consciously entertaining purposes, may there not be something in the notion that a society exhibits goal-directed behaviour in this sense none the less?

4   *The source of functional organization*

The critic may react to this clarification of the functionalist position by claiming that although it forces him into a lengthier argument it does not alter his conclusion at all: the functionalist can *still* be shown to be treating a society as capable of consciously entertaining purposes. The 'lengthier' argument we must therefore examine.

The searching question that functionalism has to face, it begins, is that of how a society achieves its internal organization. According to the functionalist view, the elements of which a society is composed — its religious practices, for example, or its political institutions — generally speaking at least perform functions which *must* be performed if the society as such is to survive. How did it come about that such practices arose? In order to survive, so the functionalist believes, a society has to have met certain *needs*, as it were: there is a need for individuals to work together cooperatively perhaps, and another for each generation to conserve environmental resources for its successors. It is to meet such societal needs that social institutions exist, the societal functionalist declares. But the critic asks: by what mechanism are they set up? What can be responsible for bringing it about that the very institutions that perform allegedly essential social functions actually arose?

The most tempting answer is to suggest that it is the members of the society who deliberately set up the necessary institutions. Preferring to live socially, they see that for society to be possible certain patterns of behaviour on their part are called for, and they set up those patterns of behaviour accordingly. Social institutions would then be accounted for as though a society were a kind of club, provided with a formal structure by the deliberate planning of its founder members.

The difficulty, however, is that though no doubt this kind of explanation may be plausible in connection with *some* patterns of human social behaviour, with many it surely is not. Religious practices perhaps provide the best case for the critic: they are founded on beliefs about God or the gods, and one cannot imagine people coming to a decision to adopt such beliefs because of their social function. One cannot, with full awareness, *decide to believe* something as a means to an end; and a man who became convinced that the whole point of religion was, let us imagine, to foster emotional bonds between members of the society would surely be bound to give up any religious beliefs he might have had. In other cases, the argument is perhaps not so powerful, but it does seem unacceptably naïve as regards many social institutions to think of human beings consciously working out what need has to be met if their society is to survive and then setting up the institution in order to meet that need.

A second idea that the functionalist might conceivably fall back on is that a society was a kind of *artefact*, constructed by some external designer. Someone outside the society would then have imposed a structure on it, so that its functional organization would be the result of a deliberate plan. Certain changes introduced in the culture of the imported negro slaves by those exploiting them, so as to ensure that it continued to cohere in its new uncongenial context, would be an example of the appropriateness of this kind of explanation, where the 'external designer' is a foreign human being or society. But the case can hardly be typical. The suggestion, on the other hand, that the 'external designer' is God or the gods belongs to a theoretical framework that would not perhaps be countenanced today as a helpful contribution to sociology.

4.1 *Society and natural selection.*   A third account of the genesis of a society's functional organization needs to be taken much more seriously. It is the theory that the society is to be regarded not so much perhaps as a machine, as we suggested earlier, but as a *superorganism*; and that, just as we invoke the process of natural selection to explain the functional organization of the individual animal or plant, so we are able to invoke the same process to account for the internal structure of a society.

I gave a very crude picture of the theory of natural selection earlier, but a more detailed account is perhaps required in the present context. An example will help to explain how the process is supposed to work in the case of the individual organism. Suppose a type of butterfly which has light-coloured wings inhabits a region within which a heavily polluting industry starts up. The foliage upon which the butterfly tends to alight becomes begrimed with soot, and the butterflies stand out clearly against this dark background. They are easy prey to the birds that live off them. Then suppose that in a particular individual a 'mutation' occurs in the gene or genes that control its colour; its offspring develop with dark-coloured wings. The mutants will clearly merge into their background more effectively than their lighter-coloured associates, and it is the latter which will comprise the easier and therefore more frequent prey. Proportionately more dark individuals will thus survive to pass on their 'dark' genes to their offspring; and in the next generation there will be proportionately more dark individuals than before. The species as a whole will have responded adaptively to the changing environment.

This illustrates one aspect of the workings of natural selection. A more comprehensive account, though still crude, could perhaps be formulated as follows. An organism is held to develop according to instructions inherited from its parents in the form of chromosomes. In any group of animals sharing the same lifestyle there are held to be a variety of sets of developmental instructions, and accordingly members of the group will differ slightly among themselves: the group will show *variation*. This means that some individuals will be better adapted to the conditions they encounter around them than others; and because in typical natural circumstances there will not be enough resources for all individuals to live a full life-span, those that are less well adapted to their environment will be less likely to survive to, and through, sexual maturity, and less likely therefore to hand on their developmental instructions to the succeeding generation. Putting it the other way round, the new generation will be richer in the more successful developmental instructions, and the group as a whole will have become more adapted to its environment. To this scheme we must add the idea that random changes or mutations occur from time to time in the sets of developmental instructions — and we have arrived at an understanding of how 'functional organization' within the individual can arise. Chance throws up innumerable mutations which would produce features that would disrupt the efficient functioning of the individual, but such features are weeded out by natural selection. The only ones to become established are those that *do* make a functional contribution to the whole (as well as those that make no difference either way). We can understand therefore how it came about that, for the most part, the structures of an animal's body each have a function, an essential part to play in the working of the whole. But we have to remember that genetically controlled patterns of behaviour, and 'drives' or 'motivations', may be of functional value to the individual as well. It is plausible to think that an innate flight reaction, as displayed by the domestic fowl, for example, would contribute significantly to the bird's survival, as would a 'drive' to seek food or drink. Natural selection can therefore explain, in other words, how 'goal-directed behaviour' can arise.

For the complex internal organization of an animal or plant the biologist, therefore, has an explanation: the theory of natural selection. The organization is determined in the first place by the organism's developmental instructions, which in their turn are the products of natural selection during the course of the organism's evolution.

The question is: can these biological ideas help with the functionalist's problem of understanding the origins of a society's organization? Can we not invoke natural selection in the case of the development of society, and so explain how society's 'parts' came to acquire the organization they now display? We shall return to this question in a moment, but at present we must note that a disappointing No is the usual response. An insuperable objection to the idea, it is claimed, is that societies do not *die* in the way that organisms do. Physical death of the individual, literally speaking, is a condition of the operation of the process of natural selection as we have described it above. It depends on some sets of developmental instructions — the more 'adapted' ones — surviving to be passed on to the next generation, at the expense of other sets, the less well adapted, which disintegrate. Mortality, death of the individual, is the sieve that keeps back the less well-adapted development programmes and lets the more adapted through into the future.

Now for a *society* to 'die' in the biologically crucial sense would be for all its members to die together; for only in this case would a society's genetic apparatus — that is, the genetic apparatuses of all its members — disintegrate. Yet, so it is alleged, the death of a society in this sense rarely happens. Societies *change*, certainly, it is conceded; but seldom do they pass out of existence as a result of all their members dying. Western medieval society passed away, for example, but not through the death of individuals; rather, individuals changed their ways. And when an anthropologist notes the decline of a contemporary traditional society — say that of the Eskimo — he is noticing as a rule not the fact that individuals are dying but that they are giving up time-honoured practices. In the words of the anthropologist Edmund Leach, 'if a culture "dies out" it may mean no more than that Cowboys and Indians have learned to drive Cadillacs'.

Since natural selection depends on a long succession of generations, it is thus argued, the claim that this notion does not apply to societies is of crucial importance: it means that the third suggestion the functionalist might fall back on — that a society's organization might be explained by natural selection — in spite of its promise, must be rejected.

4.2 *Society as an agent.* The functionalist alleges, then, that a society's component elements are organized in such a way as to secure the continuing survival of the society as a whole. But when he is asked to explain how such an organization arises he is in difficulties. We have considered the idea that it might be attributed to the Almighty, or to the society's members, or to a process of natural selection; and we have followed the arguments that would lead us to reject all three. We have therefore to ask, is there a fourth? It is at this juncture that the critic makes his point: the only possibility left is to postulate that *the society itself somehow directs its own internal organization.* The functionalist is driven to the strange view, in other words, that a society 'recognizes its own needs' and then 'organizes itself' so that those needs are met. He is thus involved, so the critic claims, in conceiving of a society as being a kind of intelligent purposer — in believing that there is in a society, besides the individual minds of its members, a kind of 'collective intelligence' belonging to society itself, directing its internal organization in the furtherance of a preconceived goal: the goal, namely, of survival.

We arrive by another route, therefore, at the concept of a society as an *individual* as distinct from a mere collection of individuals. Moreover, it is now being suggested that the 'individual' a society is has a 'mind' capable of conscious thought and a capacity for action in its own right: so that here we have a conception, besides those discussed in the last chapter, which the sociological reductionist would wish to combat.

To many thinkers, however, not much combating seems necessary. Only expose such a conception to the light of day, they say, and it must surely be rejected as in the end unintelligible. If functionalism can indeed be convicted of treating society as somehow a kind of super-person — an agency in some sense distinct from the individual agents who make it up — it has been convicted of taking refuge in obscurity: we cannot really understand what is being said.

Functionalism is to be rejected, therefore, if one takes this line of reasoning, not principally because there is anything wrong with the idea of the 'parts' of a society being functionally organized, but because there can be no adequate explanation of how they *became* functionally organized. Through the failure of all straightforward attempts at offering such an explanation, the functionalist is supposedly driven to an *un*straightforward attempt which creates more mystery than it dispels.

5   *Group-oriented motivation*

Having tried to present the critic's case, let me sketch one way in which it could be questioned.

In order to survive, an individual organism must have its vital needs satisfied: it will need to take in nourishment, to take periodic rest, to keep within a certain temperature range, and so on. The theory of natural selection explains how behaviour directed towards meeting these needs can develop: we can understand how it comes about that an animal displays food-seeking behaviour, for example, or behaviour that tends to remove the animal from places of intense heat. Note that we do not have to suppose that organisms are *consciously aware* of needs such as these, or that they *deliberately* pursue them in their behaviour. Such a supposition — as far as very many, particularly the more lowly, organisms are concerned — would be simply absurd: very many organisms — amoeba, for example, or hydra, or the diatoms, or the bacteria — we would surely assume to be pretty well devoid of consciousness, so that we could hardly speak of them consciously realizing that they needed food for example, and then setting about securing it. If we are to speak of such organisms 'recognizing' and 'seeking to meet' their needs, we must add that the recognition and the seeking are often un- or non-conscious.

An example of non-conscious (let us use this term) recognition of need is provided by the capacity of the human infant to balance its own diet. In a well-known study, infants were fed after weaning by offering them a wide variety of different foods in different recept-acles, containing different dietary components from which they chose at will. It was found that over a reasonable length of time, without any direction, they selected a balance of foods that corres-ponded to their dietary needs. In other words, the human infant is able to determine when his diet is becoming deficient in certain respects. Though unable to explain that he is short of protein, for example, he will, if so deficient in this element, tend to concentrate on items containing it from a wide variety of alternative dishes.

Even where an organism has consciousness to a high degree and is indeed consciously pursuing a goal, he may not realize the *point* of his pursuit. An adult human being may say he feels he *wants* a certain food, for example, and think of this as the reason for his choosing or seeking it. In a way what he thinks is true; but what he may be completely unaware of is that the reason for his wanting that particular food may be that he needs it.

The general claim so far, then, is that human beings as well as other organisms sometimes direct their behaviour towards satisfying their needs without recourse to deliberation or reasoning. Ordinar-ily, we might say, they do not *work out* their biological needs and govern their behaviour in the light of their conclusions. 'Automatic mechanisms', as it were, are built in by natural selection. The suggestion I wish to put forward is that we can at least imagine the development of analogous mechanisms concerned with the needs *of the group*.

It is easy to grant, as a first step, that the survival of a group of animals might be promoted by behaviour that would work against the interests of any individual showing it. The practice of giving 'warning signals', for example, might well promote the escape and survival of the group as a whole, although involving any individual actually giving the signal in an expenditure of energy and loss of time which would militate against its own individual prospects of escape.

But though we can *conceive* of an individual's behaviour that would benefit the group to which it belonged, and though indeed we may be able to think of plausible examples like the giving of warning signals, there is an obvious difficulty in imagining how group-oriented behaviour could have arisen. For we have already stressed that natural selection, as we have so far described it, is a process that depends on the selective survival of *individual* organisms, and offers no account of how developments that make no contribution to the survival of the individual could become established. If, for example, there occurred in an individual a mutation which resulted in that individual sacrificing itself to a predator by acting as a decoy, thus securing the escape of the rest of the group, such an individual would quite clearly tend not to survive, and so tend not to pass on its 'altruistic' gene to the next generation: the mutation would thus, it seems, be quickly eliminated.

But why should natural selection not apply to *groups* of individuals as well as to individuals themselves? Can it not be supposed that groups made up of individuals displaying 'altruistic' behaviour will flourish at the expense of those where such behaviour is absent?

This is, of course, a possibility we have already considered above. The objection to it was that as far as *human* groups are concerned the idea of 'death', which is crucial for natural-selection theory, is hardly applicable. Groups or societies to which human beings belong, it was suggested, do not *die* in the sense that the theory of natural selection requires. What we have to notice now, however, is that this objection has weight only so long as we restrict our thinking to societies with which we in the industrially developed world are most familiar. If instead we turn from the modern world and think of an earlier and in some ways major phase of the human being's evolutionary history, we confront the fact that for the bulk of their existence human beings have lived in small groups which were effectively isolated from each other reproductively. Moreover, it is plausible to think of these groups as engaged in continuous competition, during which the less successful would be driven to extinction: and 'extinction' here carries the *biologically crucial sense of the concerted death of every member.* Under circumstances such as these it will be members of the more successful groups that alone hand on their genes to future generations: in other words, they are circumstances in which a process of natural selection between groups will occur.

The occurrence of selection between groups on which this argument depends is acknowledged as far as the animal world in general is concerned by at least some orthodox biologists. Behaviour that sacrifices the interest of the individual to that of the group *has* arisen during evolution, in their view, and it is to be explained in terms of 'inter-group' selection. There are others, however — unfortunately for the argument — who deny the significance of group selection. They argue not so much that the idea of group selection doesn't make sense, nor even that it hasn't to a very minor extent occurred, but that its importance must be entirely negligible. It is a debate that is still quite undecided, so that once again we are forced to leave a discussion without arriving at any very helpful conclusion. Nevertheless, perhaps a matter of principle *has* been established, or lent support, by the argument we have just been following, and that is that societal functionalism is not *necessarily* involved in the unacceptably obscure notion of a society — as distinct from any or all of its members — *somehow directing its own organization.* We have instead the possibility of natural selection, operating between the reproductively isolated local populations to which human beings belonged during the greater part of their evolutionary history, building into individuals an unconscious recognition of the needs of the group or, to put it another way, the motivation appropriate to getting the group's needs satisfied.

6 *Concluding remarks*

Societal functionalism, we should note, is not the only sort conceivable. 'Individualist' functionalism proposes that we should explain social practices in terms of the contribution they make to the survival not of the group or society but of the *individual* who engages in them — Malinowski himself seems to be defending this view rather than the 'societal' in some of the things he said. Then in recent years 'functionalism' as a title has been assumed rather confusingly by sociologists who in fact reject the assumption we began with, that functional analysis can only be applied to systems showing 'goal-directed behaviour'. For them a function is merely a 'beneficial consequence', and it has been argued that almost any scientific approach to society could be dubbed functionalist in this weak sense. From these ideas we rather arbitrarily turn to consider further and in its own right the notion that lay at the heart of our discussion of the sort of functionalism that we *did* consider: the idea of a society *evolving*.

15 Society evolving

1 *Introduction*

We have suggested that a functionalist approach to society might be defensible if we were able to accept that a society underwent a process of evolution, whereby group selection gave rise to its allegedly functional organization. Other writers, however, have turned this argument on its head. If societies are subject to evolution, it has been said, social study is wrong to dwell on the functional — or any other kind of — analysis of contemporary society. Rather, it should focus on discovering the laws that govern its development, for from these its present state would be capable of being derived by deduction. J. S. Mill puts the point like this:

> The mutual correlation between the different elements of each state of society is ... a derivative law, resulting from the laws which regulate the succession between one state of society and another; for the proximate cause of every state of society is the state of society immediately preceding it. The fundamental problem, therefore, of the social science, is to find the laws according to which any state of society produces the state which succeeds it and takes its place.

It was this line of thought that inspired the evolutionary sociology of the last century and before: the subject for study was the development — the *evolution* — of society. Then not only could its present state be understood, but its future could be predicted.

1.1 *Some examples.*   The idea that societies undergo a process of evolution is not, of course, a very specific one, and different thinkers have put forward a variety of different detailed versions. The nineteenth-century polymath Herbert Spencer was responsible for proposing perhaps the closest parallel between organic and social evolution. The latter begins, he suggested, with a small number of elementarily simple forms of society, from which arise a wider and ever-widening diversity of forms of ever-ascending orders of complexity. In other words, just as the diversity and complexity of modern animals and plants are supposed to have evolved from one or a few simple primeval organisms, so Spencer supposed that the varied and sophisticated societies of his day could trace their ancestry back to one or two ancient social systems of elementary organization.

A less ambitious thesis, but one that retains its essential interest in the present context, leaves out any reference to modern societies having shared roots and speaks merely of a course of development through which all societies must pass. The view of Auguste Comte, another of the spirits behind modern sociology, was of this kind. Any society necessarily passes through three stages, according to him. First, essential for the setting up of primitive social groups is a period of *militarism*: the society is bound together by force and fear. In the next stage — the 'legal' — these factors are replaced by respect for the law and constitution. Finally, the ultimate stage of industrial organization is attained, where the ruler is science. Plato was another thinker who held that the history of a society was in outline fixed. In the beginning, according to him, a society is ruled by the 'god-like' man — the king; this is followed by a period in which the society is dominated by noblemen who seek honour and fame; then rule by the rich families sets in; then rule by the many — democracy; and finally tyranny. The conception is thus of the same sort as Comte's — though with the big difference that, whereas the latter thought of a society as *improving* as time passed, Plato thought of it as degenerating. Both believed that there were laws governing the evolution of society, but Plato thought the laws were of decay, leading social life further and further away from the ideal form of society that existed in the beginning.

1.2 *W. W. Rostow.*   A much more recent theory of the same general kind, and one that because of its continuing influence we shall dwell on a little, is the picture of economic development put forward by the contemporary economic historian W. W. Rostow. Since it is not entirely clear how literally we are to take his suggestions, it may be best to say that Rostow develops a *model* for development to which the actual histories of societies more or less approximate. The model has five stages.

The initial condition is that of the 'traditional' society, characterized by a dispersed population living precariously, close to the soil. The social structure is hierarchical, political power decentralized, the notion of 'progress' absent from conceptions of the future. Societies that conform to this pattern differ enormously in other ways — Rostow places the dynasties of China, the civilization of the Middle East and the Mediterranean as well as medieval Europe in the 'traditional' category — but their common feature is vital: they share 'a ceiling ... on the level of attainable output per head, due to the fact that the potentialities of science and technology were not available, or not systematically applied'.

At some point in the history of the model traditional society, what Rostow calls the 'preconditions for take-off' develop, and this represents the second stage. Among the preconditions are: the idea that economic progress is possible; education broadening 'to meet the needs of modern economic activity'; the coming forward of new men of 'enterprise', prepared to take risks for the sake of profits; the appearance of banks; the emergence of a centralized national state.

With the preconditions established, the economy is able to 'take-off' into sustained growth. Industries and investment expand rapidly, and so do the towns, the class of entrepreneurs, the use of natural resources and new methods of production. The *third* stage of development has been reached.

During the period following the explosive 'take-off' the technology that powered the latter is applied more and more widely. It expands beyond the industries of coal and iron and heavy engineering, for example, into machine tools, chemicals and electrical equipment. The economy grows during this fourth stage, if not steadily, at least continuously.

Eventually the leading sectors of the economy shift towards consumers' goods and services, and the *fifth* stage of high mass consumption is reached. Incomes rise to the point where people in general are able to 'consume' beyond the basic necessities, and the proportion of people in skilled or office jobs rises. Society ceases to be interested purely in the further extension of modern technology: the welfare state, for example, arises.

Though the phraseology and the details of the Rostow model may be unfamiliar, the general conception that it embodies is, I suggest, very widespread: an evolutionist picture of the world as populated by countries in various stages of 'development', all of them travelling the same road, but some further on than others.

A deep-seated aspect of this conception is the idea that the natural goal of all countries must be industrialization, and that the role of the developed nations must be to help the 'underdeveloped' in their struggle towards it. It is Rostow's detailed suggestion, of course, that the way to induce development in a 'traditional' or 'transitional' society is to supply an economic push, most simply represented by the injection of capital. Rostow thus provides the rationale of what the rich part of the world thinks of itself as doing for the poor — providing it with 'aid', the capital necessary for 'take-off', after which an economy is supposed to grow under its own steam.

1.3 *Evolutionism in general.* Perhaps it will be easier with these examples before us to try to formulate in more general terms what characterizes an 'evolutionist' view. The common starting point may be said to be this: the tenet that social change as it occurs in a particular society *conforms to a fixed pattern.* An evolutionist of the type exemplified by Rostow, for example, looks at a variety of societies and discerns in the way they have changed down the ages a single pattern that is linear in form: a movement towards greater 'productivity'. On the basis of what he thinks he sees he concludes that there is indeed one fixed path followed by societies, and that therefore, if one identifies the point on the path reached by a particular society, one is able to predict its general development from that point.

If we characterize 'evolutionists' as seeing a fixed pattern in the social change exhibited by 'societies', however, we must interpret 'societies' rather widely. For one of the best examples of an evolutionist, Herbert Spencer — as we have seen — held that the fixed pattern was displayed not only by individual societies or cultures but by the development of mankind as a whole; and another remarkable writer, the twentieth-century philosopher-historian Arnold Toynbee, associated a fixed pattern not so much with individual societies as with whole *civilizations.* The civilizations of the West, of Greece and Rome, of Islam, of orthodox Christianity and seventeen other fully developed civilizations that Toynbee identifies all followed the same path, he held — though the path did not lead straight down the garden, as in Rostow's picture, but *round*, meeting up with itself after a complete circuit: to change the metaphor, civilizations arise, flourish and ultimately decline.

2 *Criticisms*

The most straightforward criticism of an evolutionist theory is that it does not fit the facts. Against Rostow, for example, cases are cited of countries that have *begun* what he would have to call 'self-sustaining growth' only to suffer subsequent collapse. However, defenders of evolutionary schemes have a way of setting aside particular counter-examples of this kind as somehow negligible. Rostow speaks of the five-stages-of-growth analysis as only an 'arbitrary and limited way' of looking at history — as not, in any 'absolute sense, a correct way' — and seems in these remarks to be attempting to deflect the objection that there are in fact plenty of cases that seem to show that his analysis is not *correct*. One critic — J. M. Culbertson — expresses his frustration like this: '[Rostow] seems willing to use [the ideas of his theory] as a basis for generalization without accepting the burden of establishing their general validity.' What we have here, however, in the resilience of the evolutionary view to empirical counter-evidence is nothing unique. If one *wishes* to retain a theory one can always find ways of explaining away what is presented by the opposition as clear disproof. It is nevertheless true, perhaps, that because of their enormous sweep — dealing as they do with the histories of entire cultures or civilizations and necessarily employing categories of vast generality — evolutionist views are less vulnerable than many other types of theory to the impact of empirically established evidence.

To objections of an empirical character, evolutionism's most determined critic, the contemporary philosopher Karl Popper, adds objections of principle. He begins by stressing what he sees as the fundamental doctrine of what we are calling evolutionism: the doctrine that, because social change within a society follows a fixed pattern, it is capable of being *predicted*. The evolutionist position thus implies that a society's history could in principle be written in advance. Approaches to society that concentrate on these predictive possibilities — and Popper thinks that this is generally true of what we are calling evolutionism — Popper labels 'historicist': 'an approach to the social sciences which assumes that *historical prediction* is their principal aim, and which assumes that this aim is attainable by discovering the "rhythms" or the "patterns", the "laws" or the "trends" that underline the evolution of history'.

A first objection to 'historicism' raised by Popper is that the evidence for the existence of fixed patterns of social development can never be more than absurdly weak. On the one hand, if it is claimed as by Spencer that the fixed pattern is being pursued by mankind as a whole, there is only *one* case to support this; since mankind has developed just the once, how can that single process serve to establish that there is a law of development which *must* be followed in the future? On the other hand, Popper considers the alternative evolutionist view that development has proceeded more than once — that there is one pattern but that it is pursued separately by every society (or civilization, as in Toynbee). Popper's comment here is brief, but he clearly thinks it sufficient: the histories of different societies are *so* different from each other that deriving a single pattern from them is absurd.

A second objection to 'historicism' Popper thinks even more conclusive. The very idea of predicting the course of a society's development he thinks is based on a demonstrable mistake. For we must agree, he argues, that change in a society is often influenced by its members' acquisition of new knowledge. The course of our own society, for example, has surely been influenced by the invention of the steam engine, and by the 'discovery' of North America, and by our determination of the structure of the carbon atom. (These are not Popper's examples.) But if there is one thing we *cannot* know now, it is what we shall only *come to know* in the future. To anticipate an invention is to make it. It follows, Popper concludes, that predicting the course of social change in the future is impossible, and 'historicism' stands refuted.

3 *Political implications*

We have approached evolutionism out of an interest in its implications for the conduct of social study, and Popper too mounts his critique partly out of this concern. But he has another reason too, which is of great importance. It has to do with the *political* implications of the evolutionist view.

If the evolutionist is right — if social change occurs in conformity with some fixed pattern — it would seem to follow that the future of any society is as fixed as its past. Human responsibility is thus denied: whatever change a society undergoes must be seen as the product of the determinate historical process, in which the individual is powerless to intervene. Thus are we confronted with an idea that affects human responsibilities in the deepest possible way. Accept the idea and one must also accept that attempts to influence the course of events, to oppose unwelcome change, to bring in reforms or, even more, to inspire revolutions are entirely pointless. According to this view, 'politics are impotent', as Popper puts it.

It is clear that political activists will find such an enervating implication extremely uncongenial. It stifles revolutionary and reactionary passions alike, encouraging those who might otherwise be fighting for better things to do nothing, and weakening the opposition to what may be seen as evil forces in society by lulling people into an allegedly false fatalism.

4 *Marxism*

We can well understand the political dangers, then, of doctrines that declare the course of human history to be determined by laws of development which leave no room for human responsibility, and we could well understand a political attack on them on this account. It is when we realize that Popper's chief target is what he characterizes as the 'historicist' theory known as *Marxism*, however, that the situation loses its clarity. For even those who know very little about Marxism know that the very last thing this particular theory of social change has done is to castrate would-be revolutionaries. So far from anaesthetizing people into fatalistic apathy, it has surely engaged them deeply, one way or another, in revolutionary struggle.

Nevertheless Popper is by no means alone in interpreting Marx as holding that mankind has pursued and will inevitably pursue a fixed pattern of development. The view that Marx is an 'evolutionist', in other words, is not at all uncommon, and Marxism thus becomes one of the most important evolutionary theories of society ever put forward.

It certainly looks at first sight as though Marx analyses social development into stages in a thoroughly evolutionist way. He first identifies a tribal condition, in which the structure is little more than an extension of that of the family and the necessities of life are met by hunting and fishing, by cattle breeding or by agriculture. When several tribal units unite to form a city, a second stage is reached, in which the necessary productive labour is performed by slaves. The third stage is represented by feudalism: slaves are replaced in the country by an enserfed small peasantry and in the towns by journeymen; their productive activity is limited to small-scale and unsophisticated cultivation of land, and handicraft industry. Out of feudalism emerges capitalism, with production being performed largely with the use of machines and society divided into those who own the machines and those who operate them: the bourgeoisie and the proletariat.

It is easy to think of Marx's historical analysis here as meant to apply to the development of all societies — which would lend strong support to the idea that his approach *is* 'historicist'; but although some of his statements seem indeed to commit him to the general claim, elsewhere he explicitly repudiates it. He puts his analysis forward, he says, as an account of *Western European* development only, and points out that, for equivalent accounts to be given of other societies or cultures, separate detailed studies would have to be made.

Nevertheless, Marx does not leave the student of other societies without guidance. He is by no means content to describe the stages of Western European development and leave it at that. He puts forward general principles of development which I think it is clear *are* meant to be universal, so that any detailed study of a particular society's development would be a matter, according to Marx, of applying these to a particular case. In other words, he describes the *mechanism* by which he thinks social change occurs. To judge whether he is indeed a 'historicist', therefore, we must consider this 'mechanism' to see whether it leaves room for human responsibility.

4.1 *The mechanism of historical change.* From the terms we have already used its character will be already clear. The successive types of Western European society were identified by their methods of solving the problem of producing what men needed to live: this reflects Marx's absolutely basic contention that the most fundamental activity of human beings was their acquiring food and other material necessities of existence. It is, thinks Marx, the way that a society organizes itself in this respect that determines its other, less basic characteristics; and it is consequently change in this aspect of its life that leads to change in the society as a whole and thus determines its historical course.

But in that case, it may be asked, how is change in the economic organization of a society initiated? The motivating force, according to Marx, is man's ceaseless struggle to meet his human needs. In the most primitive stages he lives for ever on the brink of disaster: the productive forces at his command are capable of generating only the most basic necessities — and only if his life is one of almost continuous labour. With time, however, ways are found of increasing productivity. In the case of Western Europe, as we have already seen, tribes band together to form larger groups and a slave economy becomes possible. Eventually the struggle to expand the forces of production results in the development of the machine, and with it the promise for all men of emancipation from incessant toil.

To each stage in such a progression there corresponds a particular economic organization — a particular set of relations between people involved in the productive process and each other, between them and the tools or machines they use, between the producers and those members of the society who are *not* productive. These relations define the basic character of the society.

Although we can speak of the development of production techniques as passing through a discrete number of *stages*, however — for example, from those characteristic of tribal forms, through those of slave-based economics and feudalism to those of capitalism —

their development is in a sense continuous. During any particular stage the struggle to create ever more powerful productive arrangements continues, with the result that the relations of production on which the society is built are doomed from the start. For gradually a tension develops between the relations of production and the increasingly incompatible forces of production, until in the end there is a crisis. The existing relations of production weaken under the strain, the social fabric is torn asunder, and a new set of relations compatible with the developed productive forces, together with the new social structure they imply, comes into being: a new form of society is born.

This process will become clearer if I illustrate it. Let me do so by reference to the case which most interested Marx: the approaching collapse, as he thought, of capitalism.

Under mature capitalism there is the starkly simply situation, according to Marx, of two great classes of people locked in mortal combat. On the one hand are those whose labour sustains the whole system, the proletariat, and on the other are the bourgeoisie, who extort their wealth from the workers simply by charging them for access to the means of production. In mankind's eternal struggle for ever greater productive efficiency, however, and in the individual owner's struggle to survive, there arises a ceaseless quest for greater production and greater profit. With ever-increasing competition between owners, the number of bankrupt concerns grows, and ownership falls into fewer and fewer hands. As production for profit's sake increases, and worker's wages for profit's sake remain at subsistence level, there is nobody to buy the goods produced. There occurs a 'crisis of overproduction'. Prices plummet, businesses go bankrupt, the misery of the masses increases. But, more important, after this process has repeated itself a number of times with ever-increasing effect, the masses come to recognize the *roots* of their misery: they recognize the source of their oppression in the capitalist mode of production. At last they rise and it is swept away.

One stage of development succeeds another, then, in Marx's vision, each brought into being by the struggle to meet human beings' needs more efficiently, each registering a little progress in its economic and hence social structure, each swept away when in its turn it begins to constrain instead of nurture the selfsame forces of expanding productivity.

4.2 *Possible interpretations.* Is Marx's account, then, a 'historicist' one? We should be clear that the mere fact that he postulates laws of social change is not enough to make him one. There could be such laws and men still be responsible for their own future. Suppose, for example, it were a law that full employment in a capitalist economy is impossible without inflation. That would be a law governing social change, but it would tell us nothing *on its own* about the future course of capitalism. What it would tell us would be that, if politicians (within capitalism) brought about full employment, inflation would follow. But on the question of what choices politicians will actually make it has nothing to say.

This situation exactly parallels the case in natural science. The law that iron melts at 1535°C tells us nothing on its own about the future course of the world — though if one adds to it the proposition that the temperature inside a particular iron furnace will within five minutes surpass that melting point, the disintegration of the installation may then be predicted.

Popper clarifies this point by saying that there are really two sorts of prediction: *categorical* prediction, or 'prophecy', which declares what as a matter of fact is going to happen in the future; and *hypothetical* prediction, saying what will happen *if* certain conditions come about. Saying that capitalism will collapse within the next fifty years is then a categorical prediction; saying that if unemployment is eliminated inflation will develop is said to be hypothetical.

One may accept, then, that Marx puts forward laws of social change without ceding that he does indeed belong to the historicist camp. For by definition the historicist is not content with hypothetical predictions; he is concerned to *prophesy*, to *foretell* — to predict in *categorical* terms.

With this clear, I think the picture we have presented of Marx's conception of historical change *does* exonerate him from the charge of historicism and makes sense of the importance he apparently attached to practical action. The situation, from this point of view, could perhaps be described as follows. Marx is seen by his (Popperian) critics as contending that a society is a kind of economic machine, to which human beings belong as components. Even if they have wills of their own, the working of the machine is indifferent to them. They go through their movements in response to economic 'forces' which they are powerless to resist. It is on this construal that any attempt to inspire people to political action seems silly.

But an alternative would be to think of Marx's economic principles as constituting not a machine to which human beings belong but a building within which human beings live. Their actions would then be limited by an economic 'framework' but not determined by economic 'forces'. What is more, this alternative conception allows us to conceive of an individual's actions having an impact on the framework, so that the framework encountered by people coming afterwards would have been modified, created even, by human activity in the past.

Such an interpretation seems inadequate as it stands, however, since it offers no explanation for the *directional* character that Marx discerned in social change. He thought, as I have tried to make plain, that down the ages a particular society changed *in a particular direction* — in fact, towards greater productivity. And, indeed, he seems undeniably to have held that society would *go on* changing in this direction, at least until after the revolution. The idea of individuals making political decisions within a constraining framework of economic conditions doesn't seem to offer any explanation of this at all.

What if we add the idea, however, that throughout history people have been *pursuing* greater productivity? What if it is held that people throughout the ages have resented the wearisome toil that has mostly been their lot, and have sought and exploited every opportunity to ameliorate that condition? Would this not give social change a direction? And would we not then have an account of the evolution of society which reconciled the existence of a fixed pattern with human responsibility? For then it would be the very exercise of responsibility — people's pursuit of a rational objective — which, constrained by the economic framework, generated the evolutionary pattern. So it might be argued. Marx's view would then be that the pattern discernible in the history of any given society would be generated by human beings, in their continuing pursuit of greater productivity, determining their actions not in a vacuum but within a framework shaped by generations of human activity in the past, and one which the present generation modifies in its turn.

5 Closing remarks

Absolutely the most important part of the discussion we have just been conducting is surely the issue of whether people are the mere playthings of forces beyond human control or instead play a part in determining their own futures. For on that depends our approach to all the big problems that beset us. But relative to the topic of this book the earlier question of the proper approach in social study is important as well.

We began with the once influential idea that it is on the principles that govern social change that the sociologist should concentrate, rather than on analysing a given social state of affairs at one particular time. Understand the 'laws of development', said Mill, and states can be deduced.

No such laws, it must be said, seem to have been established, and though that might be because sociologists have not given themselves to the task with sufficient devotion one may be tempted to agree rather with Popper's conclusion that the methodology of evolutionism in this sense is one 'which does not bear any fruit'. But we have also offered the suggestion that it is possible to embrace a form of evolutionism which does *not* involve the idea of 'deducing' present states of society from past ones, and of predicting future developments on the basis of the present.

The methodological importance of such a possibility is that there would be no redundancy in studying contemporary society *as well as* its development: the former would not simply be unnecessary so long as the latter were being pursued. Its political importance is nevertheless even greater, for there would then be no contradiction between the theory that society evolves in a particular direction and the idea that human beings have a measure of responsibility for their own destiny.

Notes

Chapter 2 Man as a machine

1 *Introduction*
A layman's introduction to cybernetics is provided by F. H. George, *Automation, Cybernetics and Society*.

§ *Michie reference.* Donald Michie, 'Computer — Servant or Master?' During the few years that have elapsed since this passage was written, there have of course been further advances. Mike Apter's *The Computer Simulation of Behaviour*, a beautifully lucid review, brings the account a little further up to date and provides an intelligible, fascinating survey of the field.

§ *Mechanism in Greek Thought.* See e.g. G. S. Kirk and J. E. Raven, *The Pre-Socratic Philosophers*, pp. 420-3.

2 *Cartesian mechanism*
§ *René Descartes* (1596-1650). Often claimed to be the father of modern philosophy, and was certainly implicated in the birth of modern science. A mathematician of the first importance. His writings are their own best introduction, so long as one bears in mind the context in which he worked. G. E. M. Anscombe and P. T. Geach have made a generally useful selection of Descartes's writings in *Descartes' Philosophical Writings*. Kenny's *Descartes* is a fine but not elementary commentary.

3 *Determinism*

3.1 *A religious objection*

For an account of one orthodoxy within mainstream Christian theology, see Charles Gore, *The Religion of the Church*.

3.2 *An ethical objection*

A great deal has been written recently on the presuppositions of ethical concepts. For a clear discussion, see D. J. O'Connor, *Free Will*, pp. 23-33. Further guidance will be found there.

3.3 *Freedom*

The thesis that human freedom and determinism are incompatible has also been much debated. See e.g. O'Connor's *Free Will*, ch. 8.

§ *Laplace* (1749-1827).   Mathematician and theoretical astronomer, Laplace has been called the 'Newton' of France. The quotation I borrow from E. Nagel, *The Structure of Science*, p. 281, footnote.

4 *Indeterminism*

As a way into the very difficult matter of indeterminism in physics, see e.g. E. Nagel, *The Structure of Science*, pp. 293-316 (and see below, note to Chapter 7, section 3).

§ *Low predictability of organisms.*   The argument that we should expect organisms simply as physical systems to be relatively unpredictable was mounted by Bohr's paper 'Light and Life'.

2.2

5 *Materialism*

§ *'Entelechy'.*   See H. Driesch, *The Science and Philosophy of the Organism*, I, pp. 143-4 *inter alia*.

§

Chapter 3 Consciousness

2.3   Stimulating general introductions to the problem of the nature of the mind are the following: John Hospers, *An Introduction to Philosophical Analysis*, ch. 6, para. 20, paras A and B; Richard Taylor, *Metaphysics*, chs 1-3; Peter Laslett (ed.), *The Physical Basis of Mind*. C. D. Broad's *Mind and its Place in Nature* is a much

3   weightier contribution to the topic than the other treatments mentioned, though it is clear enough to serve as an introduction to the general field; and the same remarks probably apply to C. J. Ducasse's *Nature, Mind and Death*. Keith Campbell's *Body and Mind* is easily intelligible up to ch. 5, but difficult thereafter. It

contains a most useful bibliography. An introduction from a physiological point of view is Sir Charles Sherrington's classic *Man on his Nature*. Several anthologies are available. Flew's *Body, Mind and Death* ranges historically 'from Hippocrates to Gilbert Ryle', is lucidly organized, with a most helpful introduction and an exemplary guide to the literature.

1 *Introduction*
§ *Consciousness in computers.* There are many contributions to the question of whether this contention is valid. See e.g. Keith Gunderson, 'Robots, Consciousness and Programmed Behaviour'. Campbell has a helpful bibliography in *Body and Mind*, pp. 139-40.

2 *Dualism*
Descartes's arguments for dualism are to be found in *Meditations* II and VI; a recent defence is that by A. C. Ewing in *The Fundamental Problems of Philosophy*. The literature on the topic is large. See e.g. Keith Campbell's bibliography in *Body and Mind*, pp. 129-30.
§ *Gilbert Ryle.* A modern philosopher who was one of the leaders of what is sometimes called the 'ordinary language' school. Ryle's book attacking the conception of 'the Ghost in the Machine' is called *The Concept of Mind*, and is his most influential work. The quotation comes from pp. 11-12.

2.2 *Other minds*
An exposition of the argument appealing to analogy for the existence of other minds is provided by J. S. Mill, *An Examination of Sir William Hamilton's Philosophy* (6th ed.), pp. 243 ff.

§ 2.2.1 *The argument from analogy.* See reference under section 2.2 above.

2.3 *Introspectionism*
D. E. Broadbent provides a quick explanatory word in his excellent *Behaviour*, pp. 16-23.

3 *Logical behaviourism*
Ryle's work mentioned above, *The Concept of Mind*, is the nearest thing to a defence of logical behaviourism. Written with trenchant and elegant lucidity, it is intelligible to a beginner, but only if the *point* of the discussions is borne in mind. Ryle's

arguments receive extended criticism in the earlier chapters of H. D. Lewis's *The Elusive Mind*, and more succinctly in A. C. Ewing's 'Professor Ryle's Attack on Dualism'.

Ludwig Wittgenstein's *Philosophical Investigations*, a book that has had enormous influence on recent Anglo-Saxon philosophy, may also be read as offering a defence of logical behaviourism.

§   *'Neat sensation words'.*   See Ryle, *The Concept of Mind*, p. 201.

3.1 *Ryle's analysis of 'motive'*
To be found in *The Concept of Mind*, ch. IV. The phrase quoted comes from p. 89.

3.2 *Objections to logical behaviourism*
See references under section 3 of this chapter.

3.3 *Psychological behaviourism*
J. B. Watson's *Behaviourism* was an early rallying point for psychological behaviourism; and B. F. Skinner's *Verbal Behaviour* is another important statement. Chomsky's vigorous review of the latter has become celebrated. An interesting, clear and authoritative account of psychological behaviourism today is provided by D. E. Broadbent's *Behaviour*.

§   *Broadbent quotation.*   D. E. Broadbent, *Behaviour*, p. 41.

4 *The 'identity' hypothesis*
A classical statement of this view is U. T. Place's article 'Is Consciousness a Brain Process?'

§   *Lightning analogy.*   U. T. Place proposes this analogy in the article referred to above.

Chapter 4 Man as an animal

L. Tiger and R. Fox make an important plea for human studies to take biology more seriously in their paper 'The Zoological Perspective in Social Science'.

A more extended but still pioneering examination of biology's bearing on the study of people is Hilary Callan's book *Ethology and Society*. W.H. Thorpe's *Animal Nature and Human Nature* is also an interesting contribution.

1 *Introduction*
§   *Desmond Morris.*   A zoologist who popularized the ethological

approach to human beings chiefly through the book mentioned here, *The Naked Ape*. *The Human Zoo* and *Intimate Behaviour* were follow-ups.

§ *Konrad Lorenz.* Another scientist — one of the great pioneers of ethology — who has extrapolated findings about animals to the case of human beings and published the result in a highly readable form is Konrad Lorenz. Lorenz's chief work in this vein is *On Aggression*. Ashley Montagu has collected papers criticizing this work, as well as books by Robert Ardrey (*African Genesis* and *The Territorial Imperative*) which belong to the same genre, under the title *Man and Aggression*.

2 *Physical autonomy*

The idea that independence of the environment is importantly distinctive of man is held by the biologist C. H. Waddington, for example, in his *The Ethical Animal*.

§ *Evolution by natural selection.* I offer a fuller and less informal account later on in Chapter 14, section 4.1. For references see there.

§ *West Side Story.* An important musical of the 1950s directed by Robert Wise and Jerome Robbins, set in the uncompromisingly urban environment of New York's West Side; referred to paradoxically as a 'vivid portrait of *natural* man' in which 'we watch our animal legacy unfold its awful power' by Robert Ardrey (my italics). I borrow the quotation from Ashley Montagu's own contribution to his collection *Man and Aggression*, p. 7.

3 *Instinctive and learnt behaviour*

Texts on ethology or animal behaviour generally have some account of the distinction between 'instinctive' and 'learnt' behaviour. See e.g. John Alcock's clear and interesting *Animal Behaviour*, pp. 63-79, and ch. 9.

§ *Begging behaviour.* Experimental studies of begging behaviour in the chicks of the herring gull by Niko Tinbergen (developing an idea of F. Goethe's) have something of the status of a classic within ethology. For an introductory account and references to the original literature, see e.g. John Alcock's *Animal Behaviour*, pp. 149-51.

§ *Internal representation of the environment.* 'Animals ... sometimes behave as if they ... held a representation of the outside world in their heads, and that [sic] this representation enabled them to adapt what they do to circumstances.' Barnett, *'Instinct' and 'Intelligence'*, p. 211.

§ *Capacity for learning as the distinctive feature of the human being.* Ashley Montagu, for example, opens his collection *Culture, Man's Adaptive Dimension* with the claim that 'man alone among the forms of animated nature is the creature that has moved into an adaptive zone which is an entirely learned one' (p. v.).

§ *Absence of instincts in man.* See e.g. Ashley Montagu: 'man is man because he has no instincts, because everything he is and has become he has learned ...' (*Man and Aggression*, p. 9).

4 Trial-and-error and 'insight'

It is often difficult to know what exactly is meant by 'insight' in any particular context. W. H. Thorpe suggests a definition on p. 108 of his *Learning and Instinct in Animals*. See also Jonathan Bennett's *Rationality*, section 12 (below, note to section 5).

§ *Wolfgang Köhler* (1887-1967). One of the leaders of the *Gestalt* school of psychology. His chief work on learning in chimpanzees, for which he is famous, was published as *The Mentality of Apes*.

§ *Experiment by Tolman and Honzik.* W. H. Thorpe summarizes the experiment and provides references in *Learning and Instinct in Animals*, pp. 111-13.

§ *O. L. Zangwill.* An eminent twentieth-century psychologist. The quotation comes from his book, *An Introduction to Modern Psychology*, p. 144.

§ *C. T. Morgan.* Contemporary psychologist, author of the introductory textbook *Introduction to Psychology*. The quotation comes from p. 260.

5 Theorizing
5.1 Non-human language

There are even more impressive cases of 'animal language', of course, with important claims being made on behalf of chimpanzees and even porpoises. A survey of work on non-human communication, though not now up to date, is *Animal Communication*, edited by T. A. Sebeok.

§ *Stickleback example.* The account given here was suggested by Niko Tinbergen; see his *The Study of Instinct*, pp. 47-8.

§ *The bee's dance language.* Most of the work leading to our present understanding was carried out by Karl von Frisch. His own very readable *Bees* is perhaps the best introduction.

5.2 *Human language*

For an introduction to the very difficult but fascinating topic of the nature of human language, see J. B. Carroll's *Language and Thought*. The argument of Bennett's I refer to is developed throughout his *Rationality*, and could hardly be understood without reading the whole.

The relationship between particular statements, general statements and reasoning comes out quite well in the well-known story of the calculating horse. For some time this animal was much famed for being able to solve simple arithmetic problems set by its trainer. The trainer would write up the problem, which required a single small number as an answer, and that answer would then be tapped out by the horse with one of its front hooves. A singularly accomplished beast, people were tempted to think. For here it was doing sums; and sums involve reasoning. Now, as we have pointed out, reasoning involves making general statements. In this case the general statements were 'simple' ones like $2 + 2 = 4$, $5 - 3 = 2$. But, simple or not, the animal was apparently making them. And people were astonished because this seemed to be a case of reasoning, of general-statement-making, in an animal. The trick was, of course, that the horse was able to know when to stop by sensing involuntary, and to human beings almost imperceptible, movements on the part of the trainer. When the right number of taps had been given, the trainer would make some telltale movement of apprehension — perhaps his muscles would tense — and the canny animal would spot these and stop.

My point is only that, once we discover that the horse was simply picking up sensory clues and responding directly to them, all the mystery of his performance goes. It is now plain that his 'statements' are merely singular ones, that he is not *reasoning*, not making the general statements that reasoning involves. He is simply reacting in a reflex way to changes in his environment.

For the story of the horse see Oskar Pfungst, *Clever Hans*.

§ *Return to the rat.* See above, section 4.

6 *Learning from others*

'...everything a human being does as such he has to learn from other human beings.' Ashley Montagu, *Man and Aggression*, p. xvii.

§   *Instinctive learning.* Demonstrated only in primates; see W. H. Thorpe, *Learning and Instinct in Animals*, p. 123.

§   *E. L. Thorndike* (1874-1949). Psychologist responsible for introducing the practice of studying higher animals under laboratory conditions. For a brief account of his classical experiments and the extension by Skinner, see e.g. S. A. Barnett, *'Instinct' and 'Intelligence'*, pp. 195-7. The quotation comes from p. 196.

§   *B. F. Skinner.* Very important contemporary figure in the behaviourist school of psychology. For his theoretical stance, see D. E. Broadbent, *Behaviour*, ch. 5.

6.1 *'Tradition'*
Two excellent collections of papers by Ashley Montagu are effective introductions to the approach to human culture from, as it were, the biological point of view: *Culture and the Evolution of Man* and *Culture, Man's Adaptive Dimension*.

§   *Tradition unique to man?* The study of the Japanese macaques is reviewed by J. E. Frisch, 'Individual Behaviour and Intertroop Variability in Japanese Macaques'. Aubrey Manning cites more examples of work demonstrating non-human culture or tradition in his *An Introduction to Animal Behaviour* (2nd ed.), pp. 148-50.

Chapter 5 Meaningful behaviour

Perhaps the most influential exploration of this notion in recent years is the difficult but rewarding little book by the philosopher Peter Winch, *The Idea of a Social Science*. This belongs, however, to a strong tradition within social study which emphasizes the dimension of meaning within which men live, and which is surveyed in a helpful way by R. W. Outhwaite in his *Understanding Social Life*.

1 *Introduction*
§   *Golding's Lord of the Flies.* Readers of the novel will know that Simon's insight, for which he paid the Saviour's penalty, was to recognize that the Beast, the source of their disintegration, was not an external agent, but part of themselves.

2 *Intentions*
For the view that intentions can be regarded as causes, see e.g. Donald Davidson, 'Actions, Reasons and Causes', and

D. W. Hamlyn's 'Causality and Human Behaviour', both reprinted in *Readings in the Theory of Action*, edited by Care and Landesman.

A. I. Melden argues against the idea that intentions can be regarded as the causes of actions in chapters 8 and 9 of his influential book *Free Action* (his discussion is conducted partly in terms of *motives* but 'motive' as he uses it applies to intentions as well as to other things (p. 83)).

§ *Intention and its action not logically distinct.* The 'logical connection' argument, as it is sometimes called, is to be found, for example, in Melden's *Free Action*, p. 53, and in A. R. White's *The Philosophy of Mind*.

3 *Sense*

§ *Max Weber* (1864-1920). A powerful and prolific writer who did more than anyone else to develop the approach to society which takes its dimension of 'meaning' with deep seriousness. He held a succession of conventional academic posts. He discusses the 'meaning' of actions in his *The Theory of Social and Economic Organization*; see, for example, the extract from this work reprinted in May Brodbeck's collection *Readings in the Philosophy of the Social Sciences* (ch. I, para. I). R. W. Outhwaite provides an outline of Weber's contributions in *Understanding Social Life*, pp. 46-55.

§ *'Instinct' not informed by thought.* Cf. Marx: 'But what distinguishes the worst architect from the best of bees is this, that the architect raises his structure in imagination before he erects it in reality.' *Capital*, Vol. I (Moscow, 1961), p. 178; the larger passage from which it comes is reprinted in McLellan's *The Thought of Karl Marx*, pp. 148-9.

Our earlier discussion of instinct is relevant of course; see above, Chapter 4, section 3.

§ *Casting a vote.* Winch, *The Idea of a Social Science*, p. 49.

§ *Forgetting to post a letter.* From Freud; see Winch's *The Idea of a Social Science*, p. 47.

4 *Action*

A good introduction to philosophical thinking about action is provided by Glen Langford in his *Human Action*, which includes a useful selective guide to the literature as well as a much fuller bibliography.

§ *Actions and events.* The distinction between actions and events is a major theme of A. I. Melden's *Free Action*; see especially ch. 13.

§ *Actions and bodily movements.* For a discussion of the thought that one and the same bodily movement can represent different actions on different occasions, see Alasdair MacIntyre's 'The Antecedents of Action'.

5 *Actions and rules*

Langford has a helpful section called 'The rule-following purposive model [of action]', in *Human Action*, III, section 7, pp. 44-7.

§ *Meaning and rules.* Peter Winch did much to stimulate discussion on this theme with his *The Idea of a Social Science.*

Valuable contributions to the discussion provoked by Winch's book include the symposium by Alasdair MacIntyre and David Bell with the same title, and MacIntyre's 'A Mistake about Causality in Social Science'.

§ *Actions are rule-governed bodily movements.* It is clear that this idea gives us a ready account of how the same bodily movement need not always constitute the same action: it will depend on the particular set of rules that is being applied.

§ *Money example.* This comes from Weber. For the reference see Winch, *The Idea of a Social Science,* p. 49.

6 *Rules, words and understanding*

A discussion of the relationship between the meaning of words and rules is offered by W. P. Alston in his *Philosophy of Language*, pp. 41-4.

§ *Learning rules relating words to circumstances.* Our earlier discussion of language in Chapter 4 is relevant.

Chapter 6 The framework of experience

The general issue of 'conceptual relativism' is the chief topic of Roger Trigg's introductory book *Reason and Commitment*, which is weakened, I think, by the fact that the author seems never to have felt the attraction that relativism exerts.

Steven Lukes provides a more advanced, much briefer discussion in 'Relativism: Cognitive and Moral'. An influential discussion by an anthropologist is chapter 5 of John Beattie's *Other Cultures*, which is generally trenchant, clear and stimulating, written for the non-specialist. Two collections of interesting and influential papers on this topic are: *Modes of Thought: Essays on Thinking in Western and Non-Western Societies*, edited by Robin Horton and Ruth Finnegan, and *Rationality*, edited by Bryan Wilson. An introduction from the perspective of psychology is *Culture and Thought* by Michael Cole and Sylvia Scribner; and from the same viewpoint there is also Barbara Lloyd's *Perception and Cognition*.

An important argument behind recent ideas of conceptual relativism, not developed here, is that concepts are given their sense by their role in a way of living, and, since ways of living differ, so do concepts. The inspiration for this argument is in the twentieth-century philosopher Wittgenstein, and the best development of it in Peter Winch's 'On Understanding a Primitive Society'. For a perceptive critique of Winch's paper, see H. O. Mounce, 'Understanding a Primitive Society'.

1 *Introduction: a visual analogy*
§ *Tabula rasa.* For an account of this conception, see R. I. Aaron's *John Locke*, p. 114 and footnote.
§ *Learning to see after congenital blindness.* An extended treatment of this topic is given in M. van Senden's *Space and Sight*.
§ *Gombrich's discussion.* This is to be found in *Art and Illusion*, ch. II.
§ *Bruce quotation.* Borrowed from Gombrich, *Art and Illusion*, p. 71.
§ *Gombrich quotation.* *Art and Illusion*, p. 76.

2 *Experience structured by concepts*
The pre-eminent philosopher Immanuel Kant (1724-1804) was the thinker with whom the conception of human experience as structured by our conceptual framework is most importantly associated. His own writings (*The Critique of Pure Reason* is the most relevant) are generally very difficult.
§ *Gombrich quotation.* *Art and Illusion*, p. 78.

2.1 *Anthropological understanding*
John Beattie provides a clear and succinct discussion of the nature of anthropology in Part One of his *Other Cultures*.
§ *Needham quotations.* Needham's 'Introduction' to *Primitive Classification* by Durkheim and Mauss, pp. vii-viii.

2.2 *The experience of time*
§ *Benjamin Lee Whorf* (1897-1941). Combined a successful career in fire insurance with extensive studies into the nature of

language and its relation to thought — studies that were strikingly imaginative and stimulating.

The example of time concepts developed here is taken from a collection of his papers published under the title *Language, Thought and Reality*, ed. J. B. Carroll, pp. 151-2 *inter alia* (the editor provides fascinating biographical details of Whorf in his Introduction). Although I try to explain the example of different time concepts here, I must make it clear that I don't fully understand it myself.

§   *The 'Sapir-Whorf hypothesis'*.   One formulation of this is that it asserts 'the relativity of all conceptual systems, ours included, and their dependence upon a language', and maintains that 'all observers are not led by the same physical evidence to the same picture of the universe, unless their linguistic backgrounds are similar, or can in some way be calibrated'. (Whorf, in *Language, Thought and Reality*, ed. J. B. Carroll, pp. 214-15.)

2.3   *Theories in science*
Kuhn's view is developed in his *The Structure of Scientific Revolutions*. Roger Trigg offers easily intelligible criticism in his *Reason and Commitment*, pp. 99-118.

§   *Experimental report*.   The picture comes from J. H. Fremlin's *Applications of Nuclear Physics*, facing page 149.

§   *Karen Horney*.   Contemporary psychoanalytical practitioner and theorist who developed important modifications to Freud's ideas. The quotation comes from *Self-Analysis*, p. 82.

2.4   *The relativity of truth*
A classical discussion of the idea that truth is relative is Plato's 'The Theaetetus'.

2.5   *The relativity of rationality*
This specific issue is discussed with penetration (but not at an introductory level) by Steven Lukes in 'Some Problems about Rationality' and by Martin Hollis in two papers: 'The Limits of Irrationality' and 'Reason and Ritual'.

§   *E. E. Evans-Pritchard*.   Twentieth-century anthropologist of major importance. For the account of the poison oracle, see *Witchcraft, Oracles and Magic among the Azande*, Part III.

§   *Francesco Sizi*.   An astronomer and contemporary of Galileo. The quotation I borrow from Hempel, *Philosophy of Natural Science*, p. 48.

§   *Galileo* (1564-1642).   Astronomer and scientist of the greatest

importance, centrally involved in the rise of modern science.
§ *C. G. Hempel.* Contemporary writer on the philosophy of
science. The quotations come from his *Philosophy of Natural
Science*, p. 48.

2.6 *The relativity of logic*
See the references in this chapter, section 2.6
§ *Principles of logic.* For a way into the question of their
nature, see e.g. John Hospers, *An Introduction to Philosophical Analysis*, ch. II.
§ *Lucien Lévy-Bruhl.* Twentieth-century anthropologist of
major importance. His views on the present question are to be
found in his book *Primitive Mentality*; the quotations in my
text I have borrowed from Steven Lukes, 'Relativism: Cognitive
and Moral', p. 166.
§ *The Nuer.* A people of central Africa and the subject of other
studies by Evans-Pritchard, e.g. *Nuer Religion*.
§ *'Twins are birds'.* The problem of interpreting this belief of
the Nuer is discussed e.g. by Evans-Pritchard in *Nuer Religion*,
ch. V.
§ *Evans-Pritchard quotation. Nuer Religion*, p. 131.

2.7 *Some difficulties*
Lukes summarizes some important arguments in his 'Relativism:
Cognitive and Moral'.

Chapter 7 The interpretation of experience

For general references, see general notes to Chapter 6 above.

1 *Introduction*
§ ' ... *it does deeply influence what one shall MAKE of them'.*
Cf. D. Z. Phillips, acknowledging the distinction but denying
the weaker claim being put forward here: 'the saint and the
atheist do not interpret the same world in different ways. They
see different worlds!' (*Faith and Philosophical Enquiry*,
p. 132); and John Beattie: 'Members of different cultures may
see the world they live in very differently. And it is not just a
matter of reaching different conclusions about the world from
the "same evidence"; the very evidence which is given to them
as members of different cultures may be different' (*Other
Cultures*, p. 75).

2   *The belief system of the Azande*
Evans-Pritchard's account of the Azande belief system and his discussion of it are to be found in his *Witchcraft, Oracles and Magic among the Azande.*

§   *Alasdair MacIntyre.*   Contemporary philosopher. The quotation comes from p. 121 of his article 'Is Understanding Religion Compatible with Believing?' as reprinted in *Faith and the Philosophers*, ed. John Hick.

3   *The principle of causality*
The thesis that the principle of causality is invulnerable to experience was defended by Kant, for example (see note to Chapter 6, section 2).

An introductory account of the main different ways of construing the causality principle is given by John Hospers in *An Introduction to Philosophical Analysis*, ch. 5, para. 16.

§   *Vinyl chloride.*   This obscure and unfamiliar — and extremely dangerous — compound steps into the limelight, when certain conditions prevail, as the talented and enormously successful *poly*vinyl chloride, or 'PVC'. Numbers of vinyl chloride molecules join up head to tail so as to form long fibre-like chains in a process called *polymerization.*

§   *The causal principle and modern physics.*   The issue is a difficult one for those inexpert in physics to explore. One way in is Sir George Thompson's 'Matter and Radiation' in Harré's collection *Scientific Thought 1900-1960.*

4   *Concluding remarks*
§   *'Empirical'.*   Concerned with observation and experiment, as contrasted with theory. For an exploration of the meaning of this important term, and of many others, see Raymond Williams's *Keywords.*

Chapter 8 Explanation and prediction

2   *The 'covering-law' thesis*
Classically stated in C. G. Hempel and P. Oppenheim's 'The Logic of Explanation'. Hempel offers a more elementary account in his *Philosophy of Natural Science*, paras 5.1 and 5.2.

3   *The 'probabilistic' modification*
Hempel explains the probabilistic case in his *Philosophy of Natural Science*, para. 5.4.

4 *Pyramidal structure of science*
An introductory account is given by J. G. Kemeny in *A Philosopher Looks at Science*, pp. 168-9.

5 *Prediction*
§ *'Later'*. See this chapter, sections 8 and 9.

6 *Social study and general laws*
A review of the debate is offered by Michael Lessnoff in *The Structure of Social Science*, ch. 4. He himself argues vigorously for the thesis that explanations in social science, in pointing to reasons, *are* quite different from natural science explanations which conform to the 'covering-law' pattern. Arguing for the opposing thesis is e.g. A. J. Ayer in his 'Man as a Subject for Science' (see esp. pp. 18-21). William Dray, in his *Philosophy of History*, offers a helpful survey (ch. 2).

7 *Social study as yielding control*
'Our scientific activity and, particularly, that which deals with the social world, is performed ... in order to acquire knowledge for mastering the world ... ' Alfred Schutz, 'The Problem of Rationality in the Social World', p. 113.
§ *Singer quotation*. Charles Singer, *A Short History of Science*, p. 1.

8 *Predictive power*
A very brief introductory word: J. Hospers, *An Introduction to Philosophical Analysis*, pp. 242-3.
§ *Friedman quotation*. M. Friedman, 'The Methodology of Positive Economics', p. 511.

9 *'Realism' of theoretical assumptions*
§ *Robbins quotation*. L. Robbins, *An Essay on the Nature and Significance of Economic Science*, pp. 78-9.
§ *Friedman quotation*. M. Friedman, 'The Methodology of Positive Economics', pp. 516-17.
§ *Ptolemy*. A simple account of the Ptolemaic 'system' is given by C. A. Russell in *The Background to Copernicus*, section 3.3.

Chapter 9 Explanation and understanding

In natural science 'we collect facts and regularities which are not understandable to us.... We shall never understand why the mercury

in the thermometer rises if the sun shines on it. ... 'Social phenomena, on the contrary, we want to understand ... ' A. Schutz, 'The
Problem of Rationality in the Social World', p. 110.

A valuable survey of different approaches within the tradition
which lays great stress on the *intelligibility* of human action is
R. W. Outhwaite's *Understanding Social Life*. The book contains a
most helpfully organized and annotated bibliography.

2 *R. D. Laing*
Contemporary psychiatrist with markedly unconventional views
derived from the existentialist and phenomenological traditions.
Laing's discussion of Kraepelin's case of 'catatonic excitement'
is to be found in R. D. Laing, *The Divided Self*, pp. 29-30. The
quotations are to be found there. (Kraepelin was a leading
figure in German psychiatry at the turn of the century.)

3 *Freud* (1856-1939)
Founder of psychoanalysis, and responsible for developing very
influential theories about, e.g., dreams, the 'unconscious',
infantile sexuality and the process of 'repression'. Richard
Wollheim's study *Freud* offers a concise, but not elementary,
introduction to Freud's thought; but Wollheim suggests that
Freud's own *Five Lectures on Psycho-Analysis* is the best way
in.
§ *The Rat Man.* For an explanation of this chilling mode of
reference, see Richard Wollheim's *Freud*, p. 131. Wollheim
subsequently offers an account of this case on pp. 131-5. It is
discussed by Freud in 'Notes upon a case of obsessional
neurosis', printed in Volume X of the *Standard Edition* of
Freud's works.
§ *Interpretations of Freud.* Several different interpretations of
Freud's accounts, including that of the Rat Man, have been
given. The contemporary philosopher Frank Cioffi's vigorous
paper 'Wishes, Symptoms and Actions' takes these differences
as its point of departure (pp. 97-8).

4 *The intelligibility of actions*
Cioffi's discussion of Veblen occurs in his paper 'Information,
Contemplation and Social Life', section II. (Thorstein Veblen
(1857-1929) was an American sociologist and economist.)
§ *Wilhelm Dilthey* (1833-1911). Professor of philosophy at
Berlin, important for his writings on the philosophical founda-
tions of social study. For an introduction to Dilthey's

contribution in this context, see Outhwaite's *Understanding Social Life*, ch. 3.
§ *Walsh quotation.* From George Walsh's Introduction to Alfred Schutz, *The Phenomenology of the Social World*, p. xvi.

5 *One use of models*
§ *Kurt Lewin's 'Field Theory'.* For a simple introduction see C. T. Morgan, *Introduction to Pyschology*, pp. 128-31. For Lewin's own words, see his *Principles of Topological Psychology*.
Lewin (1890-1947) was a German-born psychologist working in later life in the USA.

Chapter 10 Acquiring scientific knowledge

2 *Inductivism*
The most important classical statement of the problem of induction is by David Hume. See *An Enquiry Concerning the Human Understanding*, para. IV, pt II, and *A Treatise of Human Nature*, bk I, pt III, para. vi. An intelligible introduction is Bertrand Russell's *The Problems of Philosophy*, ch. 6.

3 *Hypothetico-deductivism*
Popper puts his view clearly and places it in context in the third chapter of his *Conjectures and Refutations*.
§ *Thomas Hobbes* (1588-1679). A philosopher of major importance who contributed a rigorously worked-out mechanical conception of man and society to the ferment of ideas associated with the emergence of modern science. He is most read now, however, for his political philosophy, which argues the case for a strong government with absolute authority.
The quotation comes from his most famous work, *Leviathan*, ch. 14, p. 105.
§ *Phlogiston theory.* This example is also used in this connection by J. G. Kemeny, *A Philosopher Looks at Science*, p. 176.
§ *Émile Durkheim* (1858-1917). Held the first ever French university appointment in social science and did much to give sociology its present shape. A major general study is *Durkheim* by Steven Lukes.
For Merton's construal, see R. K. Merton, *Social Theory and Social Structure*, pp. 150-3.

4 *Science as guessing*

§ *Popper quotation.*   K. R. Popper, *Objective Knowledge*, p. 13. See the passage beginning on this page and ending on p. 23 for an outline of Popper's notion of 'corroboration' which has a close bearing on these remarks.

5 *Anti-scientistic approaches*

Outhwaite's study, *Understanding Social Life*, is a valuable introduction to the approach to social study that stresses the meaningfulness of human action. Besides those writers we mention in the text, there are a variety of others, agreeing broadly in their opposition to 'scientism' (see text) though differing considerably from that point on: Dilthey, Rickert, Simmel and Weber classically, and more recently Habermas, Schutz, Cicourel and Garfinkel. Outhwaite is a helpful guide. H. P. Rickman's *Understanding and the Human Studies* may also be of use.

§ *Intentions and the 'covering-law' pattern.*   See above, Chapter 8, section 6.

§ *R. G. Collingwood.*   A rather neglected philosopher of the first half of the twentieth century. The quotation comes from one of his important and interesting works, *The Idea of History*, p. 214. The quotation from W. H. Dray comes from his clear and helpful introduction *The Philosophy of History*, p. 12.

The term used by Weber to denote the special kind of understanding that pertains to *meaningful* behaviour was *Verstehen*, which has come to serve as a label for those who share this anti-scientistic approach. For an influential attempt to give a sense to *Verstehen* which renders it acceptable to the scientistic school, see the article by Theodore Abel, 'The Operation called *Verstehen*'; and, for a further comment, Diana Leat's article 'Misunderstanding "Verstehen" '.

§ *Winch's views.*   The reference is again to *The Idea of a Social Science*.

§ *'Prayer' example.*   See Winch, *The Idea of a Social Science*, p. 87. The parable of the Pharisee and the Publican is to be found in Luke 18:19.

§ *Rules differing between cultures.*   A full understanding of Winch on this score depends on assimilating his arguments about rules being essentially social; see *The Idea of a Social Science*, ch. I, especially sections 8 and 9. For a fuller development of Winch's approach to cross-cultural understanding, see his paper 'On Understanding a Primitive Society'.

We might notice in passing the echo the present discussion finds in our earlier one (Chapter 6) about *relativism*. If actions are defined by rules which differ from culture to culture, describing one culture's way of life using the action-concepts of another is impossible.

Chapter 11 Social study and objectivity

General discussions are provided by Lessnoff in *The Structure of Social Science*, ch. 6.; Ryan, *The Philosophy of the Social Sciences*, ch. 10; Dorothy Emmet, *Rules, Roles and Relations*, ch. II; Ernest Nagel, *The Structure of Science*, ch. 13, section V; and many others.

1 *Introduction*

The question of what makes a belief a belief about a *moral* matter is introduced e.g. by Frankena in his *Ethics*, ch. I. Frankena's book also offers a helpful but disciplined way into the field of ethics in general.

Again and again in philosophy one tries to formulate a distinction — like that between moral beliefs and those which do not concern morality, made without difficulty in ordinary circumstances — and finds the task baffling. Why on earth this should be I don't know.

2 *The autonomy of values*

A clear, sensitive and balanced discussion is Dorothy Emmet's, in *Rules, Roles and Relations*, ch. III.

3 *Value judgements and arbitrariness*

§ *'Rationalist' view of ethics.* The approaches of Immanuel Kant (see above, note to Chapter 6, section 2) and the much lesser philosopher Richard Price (1723-91) serve as examples.

§ *'Moral sense' theories.* The twentieth-century philosophers G. E. Moore and H. A. Pritchard are among those taking the approach to which I am referring here. My use of the term 'moral sense' may, however, be misleading. For a different use see A. C. Garnett's *Ethics — A Critical Introduction*, p. 137.

§ *'Opting' for basic moral principles.* G. J. Warnock brings out something of the boldness of this view in attributing it to R. M. Hare; see Warnock's *Contemporary Moral Philosophy*, p. 47.

4 *Relativism*
For a clear discussion of relativism which looks to differences between cultures and which points to further reading, see Dorothy Emmet's *Rules, Roles and Relations*, ch. V.

Relativism in terms of different moral *traditions* is developed most elaborately in R. Beardsmore's *Moral Reasoning*, but the essentials are clearly delineated in the paper 'On Morality's Having a Point' by D. Z. Phillips and H. O. Mounce.

For an introductory critical discussion, see Roger Trigg, *Reason and Commitment*, pp. 66-72.

§ *Rationalist/Roman Catholic dispute.* See Phillips and Mounce, 'On Morality's Having a Point', p. 146.

5 *Social study and 'value freedom'*
The most influential statement of the thesis that social study can be 'value-free' is by Max Weber in *The Methodology of the Social Sciences*.

6 *Possible mechanisms*
For more ways in which values may enter into social inquiry, see Dorothy Emmet, *Rules, Roles and Relations*, ch. II.

§ *Definition of 'power'.* Lukes, 'Relativism: Cognitive and Moral', p. 186. One might want to criticize such a definition; but perhaps it can still be allowed to serve as the basis for the present illustration.

§ *Values presupposed by any particular study to be declared.* This is the view of Gunnar Myrdal; see his *Value in Social Theory*.

7 *Naturalist ethics*
For a survey, see J. Kemp's *Ethical Naturalism*. G. J. Warnock's *The Object of Morality* is a recent and important contribution.

§ *Bernard Campbell.* Contemporary anthropologist. The quotations come from his *Human Evolution*, p. 319.

For a critique of evolutionary theories of ethics see A. G. N. Flew's short book *Evolutionary Ethics*.

Chapter 12 Social study and bias

1 *Difficulty of social study*
§ *Economic debate.* See above, Chapter 11, section 5.

1.1 *Controlled experimentation*
For controlled experimentation in the natural and social

sciences, see E. Nagel, *The Structure of Science*, ch. 14, section I.

2 *Ideology*
For an explanation and discussion of this pregnant notion, see e.g. John Plamenatz's monograph *Ideology*. Two recent contributions are Brian Fay's *Social Theory and Political Practice* and Martin Shaw's *Marxism and Social Science*.

2.1 *The ethics of 'usury'*
For attitudes to usury in the Middle Ages, see e.g. G. A. J. Hodgett, *A Social and Economic History of Medieval Europe*.

2.2 *The rationality of 'unlimited desires'*
C. B. Macpherson discusses this notion in the course of his powerful article 'The Maximization of Democracy', reprinted as the first chapter of *Democratic Theory*, a collection of generally valuable pieces by the same author. See pp. 17-18 in particular.

2.3 *Possible mechanisms*
§ *'Functionalism'*. See below, Chapter 14.
§ *Karl Marx*. For notes on biography and introductory reading, see notes to Chapter 15, section 4.
§ *Hiring of intellectuals*. cf A. Ryan's gloss of Marx, *The Philosophy of the Social Sciences*, p. 227; and for Marx's own words (or some of them) see the Bottomore and Rubel selection, pp. 349-52.

2.4 *Bias in social study*
§ *Marxist critique of bourgeois economics*. Similarly, liberal political theory, because treated as a separable discipline, 'ignores the basic economic forces, while economics becomes a technical exercise which neglects and obscures class relations'. R. Blackburn's Introduction to *Ideology in Social Science* (of which he is editor), p. 10; the first section of this book is essentially an elaboration of the present argument.
§ *Bias among professional academics*. In an influential contribution to the question of bias, the sociologist Karl Mannheim (1867-1951) developed the thesis that the intelligentsia were indeed in the best position to arrive at an 'objective' view. Mannheim's relevant book is *Ideology and Utopia*.

Chapter 13 Society and its members

Michael Lessnoff offers his usual succinct and trenchant discussion of reductionism in the social sphere in *The Structure of Social Science*, pp. 75-83. Ryan's less systematic but equally valuable contribution constitutes chapter 8 of *The Philosophy of the Social Sciences*. Steven Lukes's article 'Methodological Individualism Reconsidered' reviews a very wide range of literature and subjects it to a challenging critique — all in a startlingly brief compass.

1 *Reductionism*
   For an actual reductionist argument conducted along the lines sketched, see the paper by P. Oppenheim and H. Putnam, 'Unity of Science as a Working Hypothesis'.
   § *J. S. Mill* (1806-73).   An infant prodigy (he began to learn Greek before he was three) who became a philosopher and economist of major importance. Belongs to the British empiricist tradition; perhaps most influential as the champion of utilitarianism in moral philosophy and of a humane liberalism in the political sphere.
      The quotation comes from *A System of Logic*, 9th ed. (II), p. 469.
   § *'In terms of facts about individuals'*.   This is Steven Lukes's way of putting it, in the pyrotechnical article referred to above, 'Methodological Individualism Reconsidered'. Here Lukes distinguishes a whole host of different doctrines that have been given this title by one thinker or another, but perhaps the definition offered in my text is the most useful.

2 *Its significance*
   § *The crowd example*. Used by Durkheim (see above, note to Chapter 10, section 3) in *The Rules of Sociological Method*, pp. 4-5.
   § *Is the 'individualism' debate worthless?*   Lukes, I take it from the article just referred to, is one who thinks so.

3 *Society as an individual*
   § *G. W. F. Hegel* (1770-1831).   Idealist philosopher of enormous standing in the nineteenth century but neglected in more recent decades. Attempted a systematic understanding of the universe, man and his history. Modern commentaries are J. N. Findlay's *Hegel: A Re-Examination* and Charles Taylor's *Hegel*.
   § *Isaiah   Berlin*.   Eminent   contemporary   philosopher.   The

quotations come from his short and stimulating introduction *Karl Marx*, pp. 51 and 54.

§ *Mussolini and Hegel*. See e.g. Burns, *Ideas in Conflict*, pp. 217-22.

§ *Berlin quotation*. *Karl Marx*, p. 54.

4 *Durkheim on the reality of society*

§ *Durkheim quotations*. *The Rules of Sociological Method*, p. 103.

§ *Example we used above*. See section 2.

5 *A parallel in biological thought*

§ *Organismic biology*. A concise account of the organismic approach is provided by Morton Beckner in the first chapter of his penetrating study *The Biological Way of Thought*.

§ *Paul Weiss*. A contemporary biclogist of 'organismic' persuasion. The quotation comes from his paper 'The Living System', p. 42.

§ *Distinctiveness of the 'social'*. Durkheim, *The Rules of Sociological Method*, chs I and V.

§ *Concluding Durkheim quotation*. *The Rules of Sociological Method*, p. 97.

Chapter 14 Society as a working system

A careful survey of the arguments by a sociologist is the third chapter of R. K. Merton's *Social Theory and Social Structure*. The best extended example of societal functionalism (see later in this note) at work is perhaps A. R. Radcliffe-Brown's *Structure and Function in Primitive Society*. Dorothy Emmet provides a balanced discussion of the weakness of functionalism in her *Function, Purpose and Powers*, ch. IV. A well-known analysis of the concept of 'function' is C. G. Hempel's paper 'The Logic of Functional Analysis'. Also relevant is the discussion of explanation in general, partly written by Hempel, 'The Logic of Explanation' (C. G. Hempel and P. Oppenheim), to which we have already referred in Chapter 8. Wide-ranging general discussions are Alan Ryan's chapter 8 of *The Philosophy of the Social Sciences* and Michael Lessnoff's chapter 5 of *The Structure of Social Science*. In my own treatment I draw heavily on an article I published in *Inquiry*, 'A Biological Approach to Sociological Functionalism', and I am grateful for permission to do so. The sort of functionalism we discuss in this chapter may be called *societal* functionalism. There are others; see the end of this chapter, section 6.

1   *Introduction*
§   *Functionalist theories of religion.*   See e.g. Susan Budd's clear and helpful survey *Sociologists and Religion*, ch. II.
§   *Bronislaw   Malinowski.*   Twentieth-century   anthropologist (and sociologist) of the first importance. Takes major responsibility for developing and defending the functionalist approach.
    The quotation comes from Malinowski's article on 'Anthropology' in the 13th ed. of *Encyclopaedia Brittanica*.
§   *Marion   Levy.*   Contemporary   sociologist.   The   quotation comes from his article on 'Functionalism' in the *Encyclopaedia of the Social Sciences*, ed. Sills.

2   *Purpose*
§   *Purpose necessarily conceived in a mind.*   W. G. Runciman, for example, writes in his *Social Sciences and Political Theory* (p. 116): '...an adequate explanation of observed behaviour in terms of goals must involve not only a description of the mechanism by which a goal is pursued but also an ascertained purpose on the part of a designated person or set of persons.'

3   *Goal-directed behaviour*
The approach of the behaviourist in psychology is eminently represented by the important work of E. C. Tolman, *Purposive Behaviour in Animals and Men*.
§   *Hydra.*   A very simple organism of the plant kingdom.
§   *'Persistence towards some end state, under varying conditions'.* R. B. Braithwaite, *Scientific Explanation*, ch. X.

4   *The source of functional organization*
§   *Social institutions not all planned.*   See Dorothy Emmet, *Function, Purpose and Powers*, pp. 85-6, for an authentic example from Evans-Pritchard's study of the Nuer. We do not explore here the idea of some members of society seeing the 'social value' of institutions such as religion and somehow duping the others into the appropriate groundless beliefs. One who defended such a proceeding was Plato — *The Republic*, bk V, 459 c, d. See also above, Chapter 12, section 2.
§   *Negro slave culture.*   See e.g. K. Stampp, *The Peculiar Institution*, pp. 156-62.

4.1   *Society and natural selection*
§   *Society as a super-organism.*   Here we have perhaps an interpretation of the anti-reductionist thesis besides those discussed in the last chapter.

§ *Natural selection.* For an introductory account, see e.g. J. M. Smith's *The Theory of Evolution.* My own cruder account is in Chapter 4, section 2.

The example of selection among butterflies is based, with simplification, on a classic study by H. B. D. Kettlewell, 'Selection Experiments on Industrial Melanism in the Lepidoptera'. An accessible account is John Alcock's, in *Animal Behaviour*, pp. 32-4.

§ *'Drives' or 'motivations'.* These concepts are very problematic. For a brief introduction, see Aubrey Manning's *An Introduction to Animal Behaviour*, pp. 54-5.

§ *The 'death' of a society.* For one statement of the argument that this is not the same as the death of an individual organism, see Dorothy Emmet, *Function, Purpose and Powers*, p. 102.

§ *Leach quotation.* E. Leach, 'Don't Say "Boo" to a Goose', pp. 153-4.

5 *Group-oriented motivation*

§ *Consciousness.* The claim that such-and-such an organism is 'devoid of consciousness' is not at all straightforward, as our earlier discussion in Chapter 3 will have made plain.

§ *Innate ability to balance diet.* See C. M. Davis, 'Self-Selection of Diet by Newly Weaned Infants'.

§ *Survival of the individual.* And 'reproductive performance', to be strict.

§ *Elimination of altruistic genes.* See e.g. J. B. S. Haldane, *The Causes of Evolution*, pp. 207-10.

§ *Societies ... in the industrially developed world.* In which context there is indeed a problem of applying at all the term 'society' in a sense in which it has a plural form; for where are the boundaries of 'our society' to be drawn?

§ *Early phase of human evolutionary development.* For a vigorous introduction to the nature of early human life, see the paper by C. F. Hockett and R. Ascher printed together with a number of comments from other authorities in Ashley Montagu's anthology *Culture, Man's Adaptive Dimension.*

§ *Recognition of the role of group selection.* V. C. Wynne-Edwards is the leading proponent of the thesis that group selection occurs and is important. See his *Animal Dispersal in Relation to Social Behaviour* for a full statement. E. O. Wilson's *Sociobiology* has also become influential. A major statement of the case against the importance of group selection is G. C. Williams's *Adaptation and Natural Selection.*

Chapter 15 Society evolving

Two articles in Eisenstadt's *Readings in Social Evolution and Development* introduce the issues arising in the notion of society evolving — E. R. Wolf's 'The Study of Evolution' and K. E. Bock's 'Evolution, Function and Change'.

1 *Introduction*
  § *Mill quotation. A System of Logic*, bk VI, ch. X, para. 2.
  § *Evolutionary sociology.* For a stimulating quick sketch of the character of sociology in the nineteenth century, see John Rex, *Discovering Sociology*, ch. 6. A fuller account is Fletcher's *The Making of Sociology*, Vol. I.

1.1 *Some examples*
  § *Herbert Spencer* (1820-1903).   Wrote on almost everything, in a semi-popular vein, but with the aim of making a serious 'synthesizing' contribution to thought. Perhaps best remembered for his sociological theorizing. A brief collection of Spencer's writings on topics of relevance here has been edited by Stanislav Andreski: *Herbert Spencer*.
  § *Auguste Comte* (1798-1857).   One of the greatest figures of sociology's early history, seeking in his writing to establish principles of rational order upon which to base society disintegrated by the Revolution. Financially rescued by J. S. Mill at one stage of his turbulent, fearless career. For an account, see Fletcher, *The Making of Sociology*, pp. 165-96.
  § *Plato* (*c.* 427-347 BC).   One of the great inspirations of Western thought. The best introduction is probably his own *The Republic*.

1.2 *W. W. Rostow*
  Twentieth-century economic historian. Rostow's theory is presented in an intelligible form in his *The Stages of Economic Growth*, which began life as lectures to undergraduates. A summary, and a damaging critique, is offered by J. M. Culbertson, *Economic Development: An Ecological Approach,* ch. 14. The Rostow quotations come from pp. 4 and 6 of his *The Stages of Economic Growth*.
  § *Development 'aid'.*   In fact, the rich West seems to take more capital out of the 'underdeveloped' world than it puts in; see e.g. Harry Magdoff, *The Age of Imperialism*, p. 198.

1.3 *Evolutionism in general*
For a general discussion of evolutionism in sociology, see
J. W. Burrow, *Evolution and Society*, and in the contemporary
context K. E. Bock's paper 'Evolution, Function and Change'.
§ *Arnold Toynbee.* Twentieth-century historian. *A Study of
History*, published in twelve volumes, was, as it were, his major
work. D. C. Somervell has provided a two-volume abridgement.

2 *Criticisms*
§ *Collapse after 'self-sustaining growth'.* See e.g. Culbertson,
Economic Development: An Ecological Approach, p. 267.
§ *Rostow quotation.* *The Stages of Economic Growth*, p. 1.
§ *Culbertson quotation.* *Economic Development*, p. 266.
§ *Popper's criticism.* Developed most singlemindedly in *The
Poverty of Historicism*. The quotation comes from this book,
p. 3; see pp. 110-11 especially for the *first* argument referred to
in the text. The *second* (the one that he thinks *refutes* 'histori-
cism') is to be found in the book's Preface. One should note
that other writers have used 'historicism' very differently from
Popper.

3 *Political implications*
Isaiah Berlin's *Historical Inevitability* offers a sustained critique
of views which see history as unfolding quite independently of
human effort.
§ *Popper quotation.* *The Open Society and its Enemies*, Vol. II,
p. 119.

4 *Marxism*
§ *Karl Marx* (1818-83). The not inconsiderable political philoso-
pher who made decisive contributions also to historical study
and the social 'sciences' generally. The best introduction to
Marx's life and thought is probably David McLellan's *Karl
Marx*. McLellan has produced a much briefer version of this
under the appropriately briefer title *Marx*, which is also useful.
Both books offer further guidance on the large literature. (The
annotated bibliography to the big work is particularly valuable.)
There are several collections of extracts from the writings of
Marx (and Engels), including *Basic Writings on Politics and
Philosophy*, ed. L. Feuer; *Selected Writings in Sociology and
Social Philosophy*, ed. T. Bottomore and M. Rubel; and *The
Thought of Karl Marx*, ed. McLellan.

§ *Stages of Western European development.* See Bottomore and Rubel, *Karl Marx: Selected Writings*, pt 2, ch. 2.

4.1 *The mechanism of historical change*
See e.g. Bottomore and Rubel's *Karl Marx: Selected Writings,* pt 1.

4.2 *Possible interpretations*
§ *Full employment and inflation.* The example of a law is borrowed from Popper, *The Poverty of Historicism*, para. 20 (p. 62, 1st ed.).

References

Details of books and articles mentioned

Aaron, R. I. *John Locke*. Oxford, Clarendon Press, 1955.

Abel, T. 'The Operation Called *Verstehen*'. *Readings in the Philosophy of Science*, ed. Feigl and Brodbeck.

Alcock, J. *Animal Behaviour*. Sunderland, Mass., Sinauer Ass., 1975.

Alston, W. P. *Philosophy of Language*. Englewood Cliffs, NJ, Prentice-Hall, 1964.

Andreski, S. *Herbert Spencer*. London, Nelson, 1972 (1st ed. 1971).

Anscombe, G. E. M., and Geach, P. T. (eds) *Descartes' Philosophical Writings*. London, Nelson, 1954.

Apter, M. J. *The Computer Simulation of Behaviour*. London, Hutchinson, 1970.

Ardrey, R. *African Genesis*. New York, Atheneum, 1961.

Ardrey, R. *The Territorial Imperative*. New York, Atheneum, 1966.

Ayer, A. J. 'Man as a Subject for Science'. In Laslett and Runciman (eds), *Philosophy, Politics and Society*. Series 3, Vol. III.

Barnett, S. A. *'Instinct' and 'Intelligence'*. London, Macgibbon & Kee, 1967.

Beardsmore, R. W. *Moral Reasoning*. London, Routledge & Kegan Paul, 1969.

Beattie, J. *Other Cultures*. London, Routledge & Kegan Paul, 1966 (1st ed. 1964).

Beckner, M. *The Biological Way of Thought*. Berkeley, University of California Press, 1968.

Bell, D. 'The Idea of a Social Science'. *Proceedings of the Aristotelian Society*, Supplementary Volume for 1967.

Bennett, J. *Kant's Analytic*. Cambridge, CUP, 1966.

Bennett, J. *Rationality*. London, Routledge & Kegan Paul, 1964.

Berlin, I. *Historical Inevitability*. London, OUP, 1954.

Berlin, I. *Karl Marx*. London, OUP, 1963 (1st ed. 1939).

Blackburn, R. (ed.) *Ideology in Social Science*. London, Fontana/Collins, 1972.

Blackburn, R. T. (ed.) *Interrelations: The Biological and Physical Sciences*. Chicago, Scott, Foresman, 1966.

Bock, K. E. 'Evolution, Function and Change'. *Readings in Social Evolution and Development,* ed. Eisenstadt.

Bohr, N. 'Light and Life'. *Interrelations: The Biological and Physical Sciences*, ed. Blackburn.

Borger, R., and Cioffi, F. (eds) *Explanation in the Behavioural Sciences*. Cambridge, CUP, 1970.

Bottomore, T., and Rubel, M. (eds) *Karl Marx: Selected Writings in Sociology and Social Philosophy*. Harmondsworth, Penguin, 1956.

Braithwaite, R. B. *Scientific Explanation*. Cambridge, CUP, 1953.

Braybrooke, D. (ed.) *Philosophical Problems of the Social Sciences*. New York, Macmillan, 1965.

Broad, C. D. *The Mind and its Place in Nature*. London, Kegan Paul, Trench, Trubner, 1925.

Broadbent, D. E. *Behaviour*. London, Methuen, 1964 (1st ed. 1961).

Brodbeck, M. (ed.) *Readings in the Philosophy of the Social Sciences*. New York, Macmillan, 1968.

Budd, S. *Sociologists and Religion*. London, Collier-Macmillan, 1973.

Burns, E. M. *Ideas in Conflict*. London, Methuen, 1963.

Burrow, J. W. *Evolution and Society*. Cambridge, CUP, 1966.

Callan, H. *Ethology and Society*. Oxford, Clarendon Press, 1970.

Campbell, B. G. *Human Evolution*. London, Heinemann, 1967.

Campbell, K. *Body and Mind*. London, Macmillan, 1971.

Care, N. S., and Landesman, C. (eds) *Readings in the Theory of Action*. Bloomington, Ind., Indiana University Press, 1968.

Carroll, J. B. *Language and Thought*. Englewood Cliffs, NJ, Prentice-Hall, 1964.

Carroll, J. B. (ed.) *Language, Thought and Reality — Selected Writings of B. J. Whorf*. Cambridge, Mass., MIT Press, 1956.

Chappell, V. C. (ed.) *The Philosophy of Mind*. Englewood Cliffs, NJ, Prentice-Hall, 1962.

Chomsky, N. Review of Skinner's *Verbal Behaviour*, in *Language*, 35 (1959).

Cioffi, F. 'Information, Contemplation and Social Life'. The Royal Institute of Philosophy Lectures, Vol. IV: *The Proper Study*.

Cioffi, F. 'Wishes, Symptoms and Actions'. *Proceedings of the Aristotelian Society*, Supplementary Volume for 1974.

Cole, M., and Scribner, S. *Culture and Thought*. New York, Wiley, 1974.

Collingwood, R. G. *The Idea of History*. Oxford, Clarendon Press, 1946.

Culbertson, J. M. *Economic Development: An Ecological Approach*. New York, Knopf, 1971.

Davidson, D. 'Actions, Reasons and Causes'. *Readings in the Theory of Action*, ed. Care and Landesman.

Davis, C. M. 'Self-Selection of Diet by Newly Weaned Infants', *Amer. J. dis. Child*, 36 (1928).

Descartes, R. *Discourse on Method and Other Writings*, trans. A. Wollaston. Harmondsworth, Penguin, 1960.

Descartes, R. *Meditation*. In Descartes, R., *Discourse on Method and Other Writings*.

Dray, W. H. *Philosophy of History*. Englewood Cliffs, NJ, Prentice-Hall, 1964.

Driesch, H. *The Science and Philosophy of the Organism*. London, Adam & Charles Black, 1908.

Ducasse, C. J. *Nature, Mind and Death*. La Salle, Open Court, 1951.

Durkheim, E. *The Rules of Sociological Method*, ed. G. E. G. Catlin, trans. S. A. Solovay and J. H. Mueller. Chicago, The Free Press, 1938 (from the 8th ed. 1st ed. 1895).

Durkheim, E. *Suicide*, ed. G. Simpson, trans. J. A. Spaulding and G. Simpson. London, Routledge & Kegan Paul, 1952 (1st ed. 1897).

Durkheim, E., and Mauss, M. *Primitive Classification*, trans. R. Needham. London, Cohen & West, 1963.

Eisenstadt, S. N. (ed.) *Readings in Social Evolution and Development*. Oxford, Pergamon Press, 1970.

Emmet, D. M. *Function, Purpose and Powers*. London, Macmillan, 1958.

Emmet, D. M. *Rules, Roles and Relation*. London, Macmillan, 1966.

Emmet, D. M., and MacIntyre, A. (eds) *Sociological Theory and Philosophical Analysis*. London, Macmillan, 1970.

Encyclopaedia Brittannica. 11th ed. Cambridge, CUP, 1910 (1st ed. 1768-71).

Encyclopedia of the Social Sciences, ed. D. L. Sills. New York, Macmillan & Free Press, 1968.

Evans-Pritchard, E. E. *Nuer Religion*. Oxford, Clarendon Press, 1940.

Evans-Pritchard, E. E. *Witchcraft, Oracles and Magic among the Azande*. Oxford, Clarendon Press, 1937.

Ewing, A. C. *The Fundamental Problems of Philosophy*. London, Routledge & Kegan Paul, 1951.

Ewing, A. C. 'Professor Ryle's Attack on Dualism'. *Clarity is not Enough*, ed. Lewis.

Fay, B. *Social Theory and Political Practice*. London, Allen & Unwin, 1975.

Feigl, H., and Scriven, M. (eds) *Minnesota Studies in the Philosophy of Science*. Vol. II. Minneapolis, University of Minnesota Press, 1958.

Feuer, L. S. (ed.) *Marx and Engels: Basic Writings on Politics and Philosophy*. London, Collins, 1969 (Fontana ed.).

Findlay, J. N. *Hegel: A Re-Examination*. London, Allen & Unwin, 1958.

Fletcher, R. *The Making of Sociology*. London, Michael Joseph, 1971.

Flew, A. G. N. *Body, Mind and Death*. New York, Macmillan, 1964.

Flew, A. G. N. *Evolutionary Ethics*. London, Macmillan, 1967.

Frankena, W. K. *Ethics*. Englewood Cliffs, NJ, Prentice-Hall, 1963.

Fremlin, J. H. *Applications of Nuclear Physics*. London, English Universities Press, 1964.

Freud, S. *Standard Edition of the Complete Psychological Works of Sigmund Freud*, ed. J. Strachey *et al.* London, Hogarth Press, 1953-64.

Freud, S. *Five Lectures on Psycho-Analysis. Standard Edition of the Complete Works*, Vol. 11.

Friedman, M. 'The Methodology of Positive Economics'. *Readings in the Philosophy of the Social Sciences*, ed. Brodbeck.

Frisch, J. E. 'Individual Behaviour and Intertroop Variability in Japanese Macaques'. *Primates: Studies in Adaptation and Variability*, ed. Jay.

Frisch, K. von. *Bees*. New York, Cornell University Press, 1950.

Gardiner, P. L. (ed.) *Theories of History*. Glencoe, Ill., The Free Press, 1959.

Garnett, A. C. *Ethics — A Critical Introduction*. New York, Ronald Press, 1960.

Gellner, E. *Legitimation of Belief*. Cambridge, CUP, 1974.

George, F. H. *Automation, Cybernetics and Society*. London, Leonard Hill, 1959.

George, F. H. *The Brain as a Computer*. Oxford, Pergamon Press, 1961.

Golding, W. *Lord of the Flies*. London, Faber, 1954.

Gombrich, E. H. *Art and Illusion*. London, Phaidon, 1960.

Gore, C. *The Religion of the Church*. London, A. R. Mowbray, 1916.

Gregory, R. *Eye and Brain*. London, Weidenfeld & Nicolson, 1966.

Gross, L. (ed.) *Symposium on Sociological Theory*. New York, Harper & Row, 1959.

Gunderson, K. 'Robots, Consciousness and Programmed Behaviour', *British Journal for the Philosophy of Science*, 19 (1968).

Haldane, J. B. S. *The Causes of Evolution*. London, Longmans, Green, 1932.

Hamlyn, D. W. 'Causality and Human Behaviour'. *Readings in the Theory of Action*, ed. Care and Landesman.

Hampshire, S. (ed.) *Philosophy of Mind*. New York, Harper & Row, 1966.

Hanfling, O. (ed.) *Fundamental Problems in Philosophy*. Oxford, Blackwell/Open University Press, 1972.

Harré, R. (ed.) *Scientific Thought 1900-1960*. Oxford, Clarendon Press, 1969.

Hempel, C. G. *Philosophy of Natural Science*. Englewood Cliffs, NJ, Prentice-Hall, 1966.

Hempel, C. G. 'The Logic of Functional Analysis'. *Symposium on Sociological Theory*, ed. Gross.

Hempel, C. G., and Oppenheim, P. 'The Logic of Explanation'. *Readings in the Philosophy of Science*, ed. Feigl and Brodbeck.

Hick, J. (ed.) *Faith and the Philosophers*. London, Macmillan, 1964.

Hobbes, T. *Leviathan*. New York, Collier Books, 1962 (1st ed. 1651).

Hodgett, G. A. J. *A Social and Economic History of Medieval Europe*. London, Methuen, 1972.

Hollis, M. 'The Limits of Irrationality'. *Rationality*, ed. Wilson.

Hollis, M. 'Reason and Ritual'. *Rationality*, ed. Wilson.

Hook, S. (ed.) *Dimensions of Mind*. New York, New York University Press, 1960.

Horney, K. *The Neurotic Personality of Our Time*. New York, W. W. Norton, 1937.

Horney, K. *Self-Analysis*. London, Routledge & Kegan Paul, 1962 (1st UK ed. 1942).

Horton, R., and Finnegan, R. (eds) *Modes of Thought: Essays on Thinking in Western and Non-Western Societies*. London, Faber, 1973.

Hospers, J. *An Introduction to Philosophical Analysis.* 2nd ed. London, Routledge & Kegan Paul, 1967 (1st ed. 1956).

Hume, D. *An Enquiry Concerning the Human Understanding*, ed. L. A. Selby-Bigge. Oxford, Clarendon Press, 1894 (1st ed. 1748 under a different title).

Hume, D. *A Treatise of Human Nature*, ed. L. A. Selby-Bigge. Oxford, Clarendon Press, 1888 (1st ed. 1739-40).

Jay, P. C. *Primates: Studies in Adaptation and Variability.* New York, Holt, Rinehart & Winston, 1968.

Kant, I. *The Critique of Pure Reason*, trans. N. Kemp Smith. London, Macmillan, 1933 (2nd impression of this ed.; 1st ed. 1781).

Kemeny, J. G. *A Philosopher Looks at Science.* Princeton, NJ, Van Nostrand, 1969.

Kemp, J. *Ethical Naturalism.* London, Macmillan, 1970.

Kenny, A. *Descartes.* New York, Random House, 1968.

Kettlewell, H. B. D. 'Selection Experiments on Industrial Melanism in the Lepidoptera', *Heredity*, 9 (1955).

Kirk, G. S., and Raven, J. E. *The Pre-Socratic Philosophers.* Cambridge, CUP, 1962.

Kneale, W. *Probability and Induction.* Oxford, Clarendon Press, 1949.

Koestler, A., and Smythies, J. R. (eds) *Beyond Reductionism.* London, Hutchinson, 1969.

Köhler, W. *The Mentality of Apes*, trans. E. Winter. London, Routledge & Kegan Paul, 1927 (from 2nd rev. ed.).

Kuhn, T. S. *The Structure of Scientific Revolutions.* Chicago, Ill., University of Chicago Press, 1962.

Lakatos, I., and Musgrave, A. (eds) *Criticism and the Growth of Knowledge.* Cambridge, CUP, 1970.

Laing, R. D. *The Divided Self.* Harmondsworth, Penguin, 1965.

Langford, G. *Human Action.* London, Macmillan, 1972.

Laslett, P. (ed.) *The Physical Basis of Mind.* Oxford, Blackwell, 1950.

Laslett, P., and Runciman, W. G. (eds) *Philosophy, Politics and Society.* Vol. II. Oxford, Blackwell, 1962. Vol. III. Oxford, Blackwell, 1967.

Leach, E. 'Don't Say "Boo" to a Goose'. *Man and Aggression,* ed. Montagu.

Leat, D. 'Misunderstanding "Verstehen"'. *Sociological Review* (1972).

Lessnoff, M. *The Structure of Social Science.* London, Allen & Unwin, 1974.

Lévy-Bruhl, L. *Primitive Mentality*, trans. L. A. Clare. London, Allen & Unwin, 1923 (1st ed. 1922).

Lewin, K. *Principles of Topological Psychology*. New York, McGraw-Hill, 1936.

Lewis, H. D. *The Elusive Mind*. London, Allen & Unwin, 1969.

Lewis, H.D. (ed.) *Clarity is not Enough*. London, Allen & Unwin, 1963.

Lloyd, B. *Perception and Cognition*. Harmondsworth, Penguin, 1972.

Lorenz, K. *On Aggression*. London, Methuen, 1967 (1st ed. 1963).

Lukes, S. *Durkheim*. London, Allen Lane, 1973.

Lukes, S. 'Methodological Individualism Reconsidered'. *Sociological Theory and Philosophical Analysis*, ed. Emmet and MacIntyre.

Lukes, S. 'On the Social Determination of Truth'. *Modes of Thought*, ed. Horton and Finnegan.

Lukes, S. 'Relativism: Cognitive and Moral', *Proceedings of the Aristotelian Society*, 48 (1974).

Lukes, S. 'Some Problems about Rationality'. *Rationality*, ed. Wilson.

MacIntyre, A. *A Short History of Ethics*. London, Routledge & Kegan Paul, 1967.

MacIntyre, A. 'The Antecedents of Action'. *British Analytical Philosophy*, ed. Williams and Montefiore.

MacIntyre, A. 'A Mistake about Causality in Social Science'. In Laslett and Runciman (eds), *Philosophy, Politics and Society,* series 3, Vol. II.

MacIntyre, A. 'The Idea of a Social Science', *Proceedings of the Aristotelian Society*, Supplementary Volume for 1967.

MacIntyre, A. 'Is Understanding Religion Compatible with Believing?' *Faith and the Philosophers*, ed. Hick.

McLellan, D. *The Thought of Karl Marx*. London, Macmillan, 1971.

McLellan, D. *Karl Marx*. London, Macmillan, 1973.

McLellan, D. *Marx*. London, Fontana, 1975.

MacPherson, C. B. *Democratic Theory*. Oxford, Clarendon Press, 1973.

Magdoff, H. *The Age of Imperialism*. New York, Monthly Review Press, 1969.

Mannheim, K. *Ideology and Utopia*, trans. L. Worth and E. Shils. London, Routledge & Kegan Paul, 1960 (1st ed. 1936).

Manning, A. *An Introduction to Animal Behaviour*. 2nd ed. London, Arnold, 1972 (1st ed. 1967).

Medawar, P. B. *The Future of Man*. London, Methuen, 1960.

Melden, A. I. *Free Action*. London, Routledge & Kegan Paul, 1961.

Merton, R. K. *Social Theory and Social Structure*. Glencoe, Ill., Free Press, 1957 (1st ed. 1949).

Michie, D. 'Computer — Servant or Master?' *Theoria to Theory*, 2 (1968).

Mill, J. S. *An Examination of Sir William Hamilton's Philosophy*. London, 1865.

Mill, J. S. *A System of Logic*. London, Longmans, Green, 1874 (1st ed. 1843).

Mills, C. W. *The Sociological Imagination*. New York, OUP, 1959.

Mitchell, G. D. *A Hundred Years of Sociology*. London, Duckworth, 1968.

Montagu, M. F. A. (ed.) *Culture and the Evolution of Man*. New York, OUP, 1962.

Montagu, M. F. A. (ed.) *Culture, Man's Adaptive Dimension*. London, OUP, 1968.

Montagu, M. F. A. (ed.) *Man and Aggression*. London, OUP, 1973.

Morgan, C. T. *Introduction to Psychology*. 2nd ed. New York, McGraw-Hill, 1961.

Morris, D. *The Human Zoo*. London, Cape, 1969.

Morris, D. *Intimate Behaviour*. London, Cape, 1971.

Morris, D. *The Naked Ape*. London, Cape, 1967.

Mounce, H. O. 'Understanding a Primitive Society', *Philosophy*, 48 (1973).

Myrdal, G. *Value in Social Theory*. London, Routledge & Kegan Paul, 1958.

Nagel, E. *The Structure of Science*. London, Routledge & Kegan Paul, 1961.

Natanson, M. (ed.) *Philosophy of the Social Sciences*. New York, Random House, 1963.

O'Connor, D. J. *Free Will*. London, Macmillan, 1972.

Oppenheim, P., and Putnam, H. 'Unity of Science as a Working Hypothesis'. *Minnesota Studies in the Philosophy of Science*, II, ed. Feigl and Scriven.

Outhwaite, R. W. *Understanding Social Life*. London, Allen & Unwin, 1974.

Pfungst, O. *Clever Hans*, ed. R. Rosenthal. New York, Holt, Rinehart & Winston, 1965.

Phillips, D. Z. *Faith and Philosophical Enquiry*. London, Routledge & Kegan Paul, 1970.

Phillips, D. Z. (ed.) *Religion and Understanding*. Oxford, Blackwell, 1967.

Phillips, D. Z., and Mounce, H. O. 'On Morality's Having a Point'. *Fundamental Problems in Philosophy*, ed. Hanfling.

Place, U. T. 'Is Consciousness a Brain Process?' *Body, Mind and Death*, ed. Flew.

Plamenatz, J. *Ideology*. London, Pall Mall, 1970.

Plato. *The Collected Dialogues of Plato*, ed. E. Hamilton and H. Cairns. Princeton, NJ, Princeton University Press, 1961.

Plato. *The Republic*. In *The Collected Dialogues of Plato*.

Plato. *The Theaetetus*. In *The Collected Dialogues of Plato*.

Popper, K. R. *Conjectures and Refutations*. London, Routledge & Kegan Paul, 1963.

Popper, K. R. *Objective Knowledge*. Oxford, Clarendon Press, 1972.

Popper, K. R. *The Open Society and its Enemies*. 5th ed. London, Routledge & Kegan Paul, 1966 (1st ed. 1945).

Popper, K. R. *The Poverty of Historicism*. London, Routledge & Kegan Paul, 1961 (1st ed. 1957).

Pratt, V. 'A Biological Approach to Sociological Functionalism', *Inquiry*, 18 (1975).

Pritchard, E. E. Evans. *See* Evans-Pritchard, E. E.

Radcliffe-Brown, A. R. *Structure and Function in Primitive Society*. London, Cohen & West, 1952.

Rex, J. *Discovering Sociology*. London, Routledge & Kegan Paul, 1973.

Rex, J. *Key Problems of Sociological Theory*. London, Routledge & Kegal Paul, 1961.

Rickman, H. P. *Understanding and the Human Studies*. London, Heinemann, 1967.

Robbins, L. *An Essay on the Nature and Significance of Economic Science*. 2nd ed. London, Macmillan, 1952 (1st ed. 1932).

Rostow, W. W. *The Stages of Economic Growth*. Cambridge, CUP, 1960.

Royal Institute of Philosophy. *The Proper Study*. London, Macmillan, 1971.

Runciman, W. G. *A Critique of Max Weber's Philosophy of Social Science*. Cambridge, CUP, 1972.

Runciman, W. G. *Social Science and Political Theory*. Cambridge, CUP, 1963.

Russell, B. *The Problems of Philosophy*. London, OUP, 1959 (1st ed. 1912).

Russell, C. A. *The Background to Copernicus*. Unit 15 of the Open University course *Renaissance and Reformation*. Bletchley, The Open University, 1972.

Ryan, A. *The Philosophy of the Social Sciences*. London, Macmillan, 1970.

Ryle, G. *The Concept of Mind.* London, Hutchinson, 1949.

Schutz, A. *The Phenomenology of the Social World*, trans. G. Walsh and F. Lehnert. London, Heinemann, 1972 (1st ed. in English 1967).

Schutz, A. 'The Problem of Rationality in the Social World'. *Sociological Theory and Philosophical Analysis*, ed. Emmet and MacIntyre.

Sebeok, T. A. (ed.) *Animal Communication.* Bloomington, Ind., Indiana University Press, 1968.

Senden, M. van. *Space and Sight*, trans. Heath. London, Methuen, 1960.

Shaw, M. *Marxism and Social Science.* London, Pluto Press, 1975.

Sheppard, P. M. *Natural Selection and Heredity.* 4th ed. London, Hutchinson, 1975 (1st ed. 1958).

Sherrington, C. *Man on his Nature.* Cambridge, CUP, 1940.

Sills, D. L. (ed.) *Encyclopedia of the Social Sciences.* New York, Macmillan and Free Press, 1968.

Singer, C. *A Short History of Science.* Oxford, Clarendon Press, 1941.

Skinner, B. F. *Verbal Behaviour.* London, Methuen, 1959.

Smith, J. M. *The Theory of Evolution.* Harmondsworth, Penguin, 1958.

Somervell, D. C. (ed.) *Toynbee's A Study of History*, abridged in 2 vols. *See* Toynbee, A.

Stace, W. T. *Mysticism and Philosophy.* London, Macmillan, 1961.

Stampp, K. *The Peculiar Institution.* New York, Knopf, 1956.

Taylor, C. *Hegel.* Cambridge, CUP, 1975.

Taylor, R. *Metaphysics.* Englewood Cliffs, NJ, Prentice-Hall, 1963.

Thorpe, W. H. *Animal Nature and Human Nature.* London, Methuen, 1974.

Thorpe, W. H. *Learning and Instinct in Animals.* London, Methuen, 1956.

Tiger, L., and Fox, R. 'The Zoological Perspective in Social Science', *Man*, 1 (1966).

Tinbergen, N. *Social Behaviour in Animals.* London, Methuen & Science Publications, 1965.

Tinbergen, N. *The Study of Instinct.* Oxford, Clarendon Press, 1951.

Tolman, E. C. *Purposive Behaviour in Animals and Men.* New York, Century, 1932.

Tolman, E. C., and Honzik, C. H. 'Insight in Rats', *University of California Publications in Psychology*, 4 (1930).

Toynbee, A. *A Study of History*, abridged in 2 vols by D. C. Somervell. London, OUP, 1934.

Trigg, R. *Reason and Commitment*. Cambridge, CUP, 1973.

Waddington, C. H. *The Ethical Animal*. London, Allen & Unwin, 1960.

Walsh, W. H. *Reason and Experience*. Oxford, Clarendon Press, 1947.

Warnock, G. J. *Contemporary Moral Philosophy*. London, Macmillan, 1967.

Warnock, G. J. *The Object of Morality*. London, Methuen, 1971.

Watson, J. B. *Behaviourism*. Chicago, Ill., University of Chicago Press, 1924.

Weber, M. *The Methodology of the Social Sciences*. Glencoe, Ill., Free Press, 1949.

Weber, M. *The Theory of Social and Economic Organization*. Glencoe, Ill., Free Press, 1964.

Weiss, P. 'The Living System: Determinism Stratified'. *Beyond Reductionism*, ed. Koestler and Smythies.

White, A. R. *The Philosophy of Mind*. New York, Random House, 1967.

Whorf, B. L. *Language, Thought and Reality*, ed. J. B. Carroll. Cambridge, Mass., MIT, 1956.

Williams, B., and Montefiore, A. (eds) *British Analytical Philosophy*. London, Routledge & Kegan Paul, 1966.

Williams, G. C. *Adaptation and Natural Selection*. Princeton, NJ, Princeton University Press, 1966.

Williams, R. *Keywords*. London, Fontana/Croom Helm, 1976.

Wilson, B. R. (ed.) *Rationality*. Oxford, Blackwell, 1970.

Wilson, E. O. *Sociobiology*. Cambridge, Mass., Harvard University Press, 1975.

Winch, P. *The Idea of a Social Science*. London, Routledge & Kegan Paul, 1958.

Winch, P. 'On Understanding a Primitive Society'. *Religion and Understanding*, ed. Phillips.

Wittgenstein, L. *Philosophical Investigations*, trans. G. E. M. Anscombe. Oxford, Blackwell, 1953.

Wollheim, R. *Freud*. London, Fontana/Collins, 1971.

Woodger, J. H. *Biological Principles*. London, Routledge & Kegan Paul, 1948.

Wynne-Edwards, V. C. *Animal Dispersion in Relation to Social Behaviour*. Edinburgh, Oliver & Boyd, 1962.

Zangwill, O. L. *An Introduction to Modern Psychology*. London, Methuen, 1962.

Some books of general relevance

1 Introductions to the philosophical aspects of social study

Brown, R. *Explanation in Social Science*. London, Routledge & Kegan Paul, 1963.

Gibson, Q. *The Logic of Social Enquiry*. London, Routledge & Kegan Paul, 1960.

Kaplan, A. *The Conduct of Inquiry — Methodology for Behavioural Sciences*. San Francisco, Chandler, 1965.

Kaufmann, F. *Methodology in the Social Sciences*. London, OUP, 1944.

Keat, R. N., and Urry, J. R. *Social Theory as Science*. London, Routledge & Kegan Paul, 1975.

Lessnoff, M. *The Structure of Social Science*. London, Allen & Unwin, 1974.

Rudner, R. S. *Philosophy of Social Science*. Englewood Cliffs, NJ, Prentice-Hall, 1966.

Ryan, A. *The Philosophy of the Social Sciences*. London, Macmillan, 1970.

Weber, M. *The Methodology of the Social Sciences*. Glencoe, Ill., Free Press, 1949.

II Introductions to the philosophy of science, which include substantial sections on social study

Cohen, M. R. *Reason and Nature*. New York, Harcourt Brace, 1931.

Frank, P. *Philosophy of Science*. Englewood Cliffs, NJ, Prentice-Hall, 1957.

Mill, J. S. *A System of Logic*. London, 1843.

Nagel, E. *The Structure of Science*. London, Routledge & Kegan Paul, 1961.

Pap, A. *Introduction to the Philosophy of Science*. Glencoe, Ill., Free Press, 1962.

Wartofsky, M. W. *Conceptual Foundations of Scientific Thought*. New York, Macmillan, 1968.

III Anthologies devoted to the philosophy of social study

Braybrooke, D. (ed.) *Philosophical Problems of the Social Sciences*. New York, Macmillan, 1965.

Brodbeck, M. (ed.) *Readings in the Philosophy of the Social Sciences*. New York, Macmillan, 1968.

Borger, R., and Cioffi, F. (eds) *Explanation in the Behavioural Sciences*. Cambridge, CUP, 1970.

Emmet, D., and MacIntyre, A. (eds) *Sociological Theory and Philosophical Analysis*. London, Macmillan, 1970.

Krimerman, L. I. (ed.) *The Nature and Scope of Social Science*. New York, Appleton-Century-Crofts, 1969.

Natanson, M. (ed.) *Philosophy of the Social Sciences*. New York, Random House, 1963.

Ryan, A. (ed.) *The Philosophy of Social Explanation*. London, OUP, 1973.

IV *Anthologies covering an area wider than ours, but including relevant pieces*

Brody, B. A. (ed.) *Readings in the Philosophy of Science*. Englewood Cliffs, NJ, Prentice-Hall, 1970.

Feigl, H., and Brodbeck, M. (eds) *Readings in the Philosophy of Science*. New York, Appleton-Century-Crofts, 1953.

Madden, E. (ed.) *The Structure of Scientific Thought*. Boston, Mass., Houghton Mifflin, 1960.

Wiener, P. P. (ed.) *Readings in the Philosophy of Science*. New York, Scribner's, 1953.

Index